W9-AHT-279

THE DEVIL OF DECOURCY ISLAND
THE BROTHER XII.

1st edition copy
Ron MacIsaac

Ron MacIsaac
Don Clark
Charles Lillard

PORCÉPIC BOOKS

Copyright © 1989 by Ronald MacIsaac, Charles Lillard and Donald Clark

All rights reserved.

No part of this book may be reproduced or transmitted in any form by any means, electronic or mechanical, including photocopying, recording or any information storage, retrieval and transmission systems now known or to be invented, without permission in writing from the publisher, except by a reviewer who may quote brief passages in a review.

This edition is published by Press Porcépic Limited, 4252 Commerce Circle, Victoria, B.C. V8Z 4M2, with the assistance of the Canada Council and the B.C. Title Assistance Program.

Canadian Cataloguing in Publication Data

MacIsaac, Ronald, 1925-
    The Brother XII

    ISBN 0-88878-286-1

    1. Brother XII. 2. Theosophists - British
Columbia - Vancouver Island - Biography. 3.
Cults - British Columbia - Vancouver Island -
History. I. Lillard, Charles, 1944-
II. Clark, Donald, 1929-   III. Title.

CT9981.B76M24 1989   299'.934'092 C90-091010-0

To the late **Donald H. Clark**
and
the late **Bruce McKelvie**

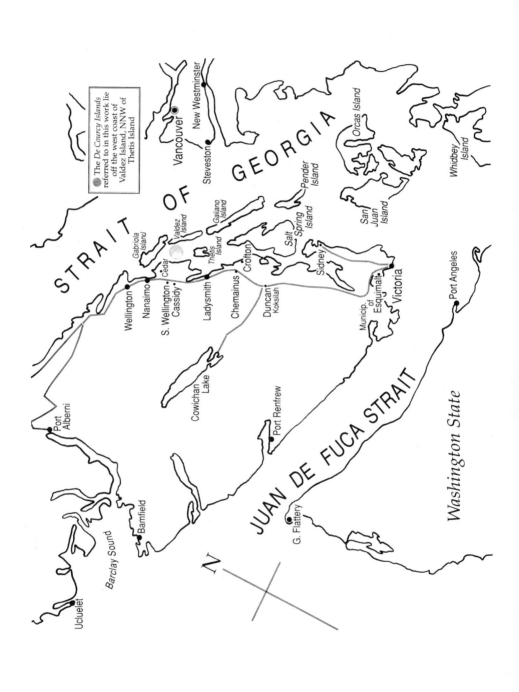

The *De Courcy Islands* referred to in this work lie off the west coast of Valdez Island, NNW of Thetis Island

STRAIT OF GEORGIA

New Westminster

Vancouver

Steveston

Orcas Island

Whidbey Island

Gabriola Island

Valdez Island

Galiano Island

Pender Island

San Juan Island

Cedar

Wellington

Nanaimo

S. Wellington · Cassidy

Thetis Island

Salt Spring Island

Ladysmith

Crofton

Sidney

Chemainus

Duncan Koksilah

Municip. of Esquimalt

Victoria

Port Angeles

Cowichan Lake

Port Alberni

Port Renfrew

Washington State

Bamfield

JUAN DE FUCA STRAIT

Barclay Sound

G. Flattery

N

Ucluelet

Table of Contents

Note

"A man will turn over half a library," said Dr. Johnson, "to make one book." And the man turning over all those volumes will probably write more than one book before he is satisfied with the result. Robert Louis Stevenson said it wasn't the first draft of a book that he minded, it was the fifth.

Let Johnson's and Stevenson's comments explain in part why this book has been presented in the first person singular, despite the fact that there are three authors.

It was a story that grew in the telling. Sparked by intrepid reporter Bruce McKelvie, in spirit at least, the research began in earnest when Dr. Donald H. Clark began collecting evidence during the 1950s; the project was continued by Clark's son, Don. Then Ron MacIsaac, working on his own, brought information, drafts and articles to the growing story of The Brother, XII. Charles Lillard then joined the above-named authors and, in turn, came up with his own manuscript.

Working behind one "I" together, they made this book.

Prelude

Twenty miles south of Nanaimo, Steve turned to me and said, "Lillard, what do you know about Brother XII?" Then he started to tell me about Brother XII, about his hidden gold and the female slaves he drove to madness and death with the help of his drug-crazed mistress Madame Zee--and how in 1933 the man and his mistress sailed off into the same silence from whence they'd stepped in 1927.

A few minutes into the story Steve waved his hand at a wooden sign hanging at the edge of the winding highway. "Cedar's down there," he said. "That's where his headquarters was; for all I know some of his people are there yet."

I remember thinking that this Brother XII, a religious con man of some sort, didn't sound like much of anything. My reaction was partly because I'd spent the winter in Vancouver and it was 1967 and the city was crawling with hippies. Bookstores that couldn't give away Alan Watts or Gurdjieff or Ouspensky or Aleister Crowley a year before suddenly couldn't keep up with the demand for their works.

Another reason for my lack of interest in XII might have been the blue-green allure of Vancouver Island itself. It was early summer, the roads were almost deserted and we were on our way to Kelsey Bay. After a musty winter, I was desperate for open country and fresh air. To hell with religious fanatics, good, bad, indifferent. Five days a week, all winter long, I'd ridden a bus through Vancouver's hippy haven on my way to the University of British Columbia; there I'd seen all the True Believers I needed to see, thank you.

But this Brother XII wouldn't leave me alone. His gold and slaves and drug-dealing were favourite topics of conversation that summer everywhere I went up and down British Columbia's coast. Within a year or two, after the interest in the drug culture began to slacken and coastal gossip was finally to other matters, Herbert Emmerson Wilson published his version of his nefarious brother's life in *Canada's False Prophet, The Notorious Brother 12.*

Not long after that brotherly snitchery, Cecil Clark and Pierre Berton each wrote brief accounts of the "false prophet" now known to be Edward Arthur Wilson. These sensational non-fiction accounts of the monstrous shapes human evil can take were followed by Jack Hodgins's *The Invention of the World,* a nationally acclaimed novel revolving around a religious leader like Brother XII who leads his flock to Vancouver Island.

Ten years later, my own *Seven Shillings a Year: A History of Vancouver Island* was published; throughout the research and the writing of it I kept meeting Brother XII. The hippies twenty years earlier had been young and idealistic; understanding them did not help me explain the black-hearted deeds of XII, a man who fleeced thousands of elderly followers only to sail away into the night, escaping law and justice. As I read and wrote my history of the island, I wished I'd listened to Steve and others more closely.

So when I was asked to work on this study of Brother XII with Don Clark and Ron MacIsaac, no one had to ask me a second time. It was my time for XII. I started assembling into one narrative all the versions of how the tale is often told--but in my delving and sleuthing, I found myself questioning our gullible and blinkered status quo. Unlike a novel, which might have a few main characters and a handful of others, this saga's roll call grew longer every day I worked. A number of those people turned out not to be who or what they first seemed, and the more questions I asked, the more questions I asked, the more questions there were. Finally, as I was getting closer and closer to something near the truth, I realized how many people, even now, were still embellishing a story that had been pretty florid from the start.

I had come full circle to explore the mystery lying behind one of the strangest passages in my first Vancouver Island notebook. "Tofino. End of the season," I'd written. "Tomorrow I fly to Vancouver. Tonight it's this lounge. With half-a-dozen others I've been listening spellbound to the beer-slinger tell story after story about Brother XII.

"His final line was so good I don't want to forget it. 'That son-of-a-bitch was so evil, when XII reached hellfire and damnation, the devil renamed a day in hell in his honour.'"

THE LEGEND

I

Order In Court

They say that Aulay MacAulay Morrison, Chief Justice of the Supreme Court of British Columbia, gavelled his court to order at eleven in the morning. It was April 2, 1933, the day secular justice would chalk up a solid victory over the spiritual crimes of Brother XII. Or so everyone prayed.

Four years earlier another adversarial situation had been very different. In the same courtroom, Brother XII's magic had stunned and floored the opposing lawyer. In agony the lawyer, T.P. Morton, admitted to Judge Beevor-Potts he had completely forgotten the subject of the case. Before anything more could be said, Morton collapsed on the hardwood floor.

Four years is a short time. Would Brother XII win again? The courtroom audience in 1933 was prepared for nothing less exciting than a duel to the death. Right versus wrong. The Law versus Black Magic. Tension mounted as spectators jammed the seating in the stuffy room to witness what was heralded as "an event in which the most amazing disclosures were to be made."

Spellbound, the audience listened as a queue of weary and embittered Aquarian Foundation loyalists, speaking in turn from the witness box, shocked and then horrified them with tales of cruelty and deprivation. One observer claimed the story he heard outrivalled old-fashioned dime novels. It had black magic, sorcery, fiendish cruelty, buried gold, fortified islands, strange invocations recovered from the ruins of Egypt and one man's domination of eight thousand souls.

No one in the audience could have realized how the balance of power before the judge was appallingly one-sided. A prominent lawyer and frequent mayor of Nanaimo, Victor B. Harrison had built a powerful case for his clients, Mary Connally and the Alfred Barleys. He planned to ask for restitution of huge sums of money that the plaintiffs had entrusted to Brother XII's care for buildings and plans that did not materialize. Further, he would petition that deeds for certain lands owned by the Aquarian Foundation be signed over to his clients and, as a final blow to Brother XII, he asked that certain monies be granted his clients to compensate for damages physical and mental.

The plaintiffs were all present, thoroughly prepared and ready to back up their testimony. Each witness was determined to add whatever fuel he or she could to the fire that would forever remove the feathers from Brother XII's celestial wings.

Barrister Frank Cunliffe stood for Brother XII and his companion, Madame Zee. In pathetic contrast to Victor Harrison, Cunliffe was alone. Brother XII and Madame Zee were not in court, nor were there any witnesses for their defence. For the hapless lawyer, it was shaping up to be a day of torment and frustration. Although some may have suspected what lay ahead, no one but Cunliffe himself knew the degree of his helplessness and the flimsiness of his evidence.

Confidential, as of yet, was his knowledge that his clients were gone, far out of reach, and with them any defence he might conceivably have presented. How they had managed the perfect get-away--what is so often the most difficult part of any crime--he did not know. But he had been paid, and once he earned his money, his day of infamy would be over.

Amazement quickly turned to dismay as the courtroom audience realized that the two were not joining their lawyer. Everyone had come to see them and there was not a man or woman there who did not expect to be entertained well and truly by Brother XII's magic. Even in their disillusioned state, his former students looked forward to a show as Brother XII played out a hand that, as always, would be held close to his chest.

Somewhat confused by Brother XII's no-show gambit, Victor Harrison called "Lady Mary" to the witness stand. The famous Mary Connally was flesh and blood; her story would damn the missing defendants, no matter where they were. Soft- spoken, gentle and generous, a southern lady in every respect, Mary Connally approached the witness stand. She told how, methodically, she had been bled of countless thousands of dollars, then, with her assets exhausted, had been subjected to abuse, forced isolation and labours that even a prisoner of war under battlefield conditions would not anticipate.

Heartbroken and exhausted by her recent ordeal, Mary Connally took the stand. The dull preliminaries were over. Now the show was ready to begin.

Few of the spectators would ever know they had already missed the most sensational part of the trial. Central to the surprise that the courtroom audience missed were Victor Harrison and Bruce McKelvie, then managing editor of *The Colonist*, Vancouver Island's leading newspaper. Joining them was the entire assemblage of Brother XII's disgruntled disciples. There was also a strange Indian charm.

A year earlier when Bruce McKelvie had been in Ottawa reporting the Imperial Conference, a letter arrived from his friend Victor Harrison. "I know you have been trying for years to obtain the truth about Brother XII," he wrote, "so I thought I would let you know that I have been retained by two members of the cult to enter suit against Wilson [Brother XII] in an effort to recover some of the money they have contributed."

McKelvie returned to Victoria, his interest piqued. Weeks went by and he heard nothing from Harrison, and there was no sign that action had been initiated. Unable to contain his curiosity, McKelvie drove to Nanaimo to learn firsthand what was happening.

Gloomily, Harrison admitted to McKelvie he did not believe he could get his clients to press their charges.

"Why?" asked the surprised McKelvie.

"Do you remember that case in the police court in 1928, and how England's [the defendant] lawyer fainted?"

McKelvie remembered very well, as he reminded Harrison. He had been in the courtroom.

"That's it," continued Harrison. "They say he was knocked over by the black magic of Egypt, and they're afraid that if they start action, they'll all be killed by similar dark powers. Then there was the disappearance, immediately after, of Bob England--and that has never been explained."

McKelvie listened, pondered, then volunteered to have a talk with Brother XII's recalcitrant disciples. He asked the lawyer where they were to be found.

"This is Monday," McKelvie said. "Better tell them I'll be there on Friday-- it's a mystical day."

Four days later McKelvie met the disciples in the house that had been Brother XII's headquarters. The room was large and empty. A chair was placed against a blank wall, and twelve more were arranged in a semicircle before McKelvie.

In dull monotones the dissidents detailed the abuses they had endured from their psychopathic messiah and his whip-wielding enforcer, Madame Zee.

If their allegiance was broken, their faith was strong. "There is nothing wrong with the religion," one said, "it is sound and true.

It's Wilson. The only thing we can believe is that he is not himself; the powers of darkness have taken control of him."

Fear of Brother XII filled each of their faces.

"Do you know," blurted out a person Bruce McKelvie did not know, "he tried to kill Mary Connally with magic last Tuesday? We know of it through occult means. She left her house and spent the night with Mrs. Barley. Bruce Crawford slept in her house, and all night he had to wrestle with the black influence."

"Yes," chimed in Crawford. "In the morning I was mentally and physically exhausted. I have hardly recovered yet."

McKelvie studied the harassed men and women carefully before posing his key question.

"This is Egyptian magic, isn't it?"

"Yes," said Painter, "the most virulent kind."

"Pooh!" snorted McKelvie, snapping his fingers. "You've forgotten the first principle of magic." .

"What's that?" several men demanded as they jumped to their feet.

"I mean just what I say," replied McKelvie. "Don't you know that where there is magic native to the soil, no foreign magic has any potency? Here you are, living on one of the sacred grounds of the Cowichans; here they made their magic; here they made their medicine; here the young men went through their warrior tests."

In later years, McKelvie enjoyed relating what happened following his brief lecture on magic. Each face, he claimed, was washed in simultaneous relief. Each member of the group thanked him, some repeatedly; as a reward they gave him a tour of the Mystery House, pointing out the cot Brother XII used when he went into his trances.

The next day the group sent a representative to Nanaimo and the offices of Victor Harrison. Mary Connally was the first to act. On October 28, 1932 in the Supreme Court of British Columbia, she challenged Brother XII's representations, which she declared were made both verbally and in writing. When he learned of this, Brother XII knew the end had come to his scheming. Mary Connally was his angel, and without her money and influence he was nothing.

On November 5, 1932 Alfred Barley filed his complaint. Others followed, but none hurt Brother XII, if he could be hurt by his memories, as much as did the defection of Barley and his wife. Having joined him in England, they had been his first disciples.

The curious who managed to crowd into the courtroom were primed for action. It was April 2, 1933. Within minutes the bailiff would call the court to order. Much to Victor Harrison's relief, everything had gone smoothly, and then--

"I went over to the courtroom a little early," McKelvie remembered, "and as I entered the building, Mr. Harrison came running up to me."

"Good Lord," he cried. "I can't get them into the courtroom."

"Is it Brother XII?"

"No, it's this damned Egyptian magic again. They say Wilson has a satellite here who's thrown a spell around the witness box, and if they step into it, they'll die."

Then McKelvie realized his mistake. When he had earlier reassured the disciples that local magic preempts foreign magic, he had localized the immunity to Cedar-by-the-Sea. Now the group found itself in a strange building nine miles from the exorcized land.

McKelvie asked Harrison to hold the judge for ten minutes.

Back in his hotel room, McKelvie dug into his suitcase for a stone labret, a lip ornament that was once the major piece of finery in a Haida woman's wardrobe. Returning to the courthouse he sought out Roger Painter.

"Come in here--I want to show you something," McKelvie whispered as he pushed the fear-struck Painter into an empty room.

"See this, Roger?" he asked, his cupped hands barely revealing the lip ornament. "It used to belong to the most famous of Haida medicine women. As long as you are in association with this charm, no power under heaven can hurt you."

Painter's face lit up and he begged McKelvie to lend him the stone.

"Lend it? Lend it? Why, man, I'd almost as soon lose my life as to lose that."

"Oh, lend it to me," Painter pleaded.

"How long?"

"Just for this case."

"Well, swear that I'll get it back," insisted McKelvie.

Painter took a solemn pledge that the charm would be returned at the end of the trial, and then hurried away to inform the others of his prize.

Years later, McKelvie remembered that every Aquarian entered the witness box holding the labret. Every man and woman looked Brother XII's lawyer in the eye while he or she answered fully and without hesitation.

II

Edward Arthur Wilson

The Canadian west coast segment of Brother XII's story begins in 1905. Eyewitnesses place him in a Dominion Express Company's office in Victoria; XII, known then only as Edward Arthur Wilson, was employed by the company as a clerk. And while in Victoria he rented a room from Peggy Reynolds, a boarding-house operator. His rooms, she'd complained, were littered with books and notepads. The man was constantly studying and writing. But as he was a likeable young man, she put up with his clutter and strange ways. She even put up with him not paying his board and room bill for weeks at a time.

"There came a time," wrote Morton L. Bennett in *The Shoulder Strap*, the official journal of the British Columbia Provincial Police, "when Wilson tired of clerking [for the Dominion Express]. He was too loyal to quit without a good reason so he told the boss that he wanted a substantial increase in salary. This was promptly refused. Mr. Wilson just as promptly tendered his resignation, which was accepted with the same alacrity." This "increase," according to Pierre Berton, was "only slightly less than that paid to the President of the Canadian Pacific Railway."

During his free time Wilson and his friend Walter Miles sailed the Strait of Georgia and Puget Sound in a small boat. They did this frequently, making trips in every direction and for widely varying periods of time until both knew every doghole and sunset beach between Seattle and Quadra Island. During these jaunts they learned how private certain spots on this coast can be. Wilson's extensive explorations took place prior to World War I, but little has changed; during the late 1970s, early in the season -- before school was out and while the weather remained too dicey for the Sunday Sailors -- there were still many coves where a man could set up a camp and not hear another human voice for days.

Most authorities placidly agree that Edward Arthur Wilson was born Julian Churton Skottowe in England about 1871. "He was the son of an Apostolic Catholic church missionary to the heathen of India's Kashmir province," wrote Paul St. Pierre. Wilson/Skottowe's mother, according to St. Pierre, whose information came from family friends, was "wholly or part a Kashmir native."

About 1885 the young man ran away to sea. In some of his tales he told how he joined the British merchant marine; other times, he claimed to have signed up with the Royal Navy.

He is known to have reached Calgary next, and there he started his career with the Dominion Express Company. People who knew him then remember him bragging about his days at sea, how he'd been a cowboy and much else besides. This was about 1900.

Herbert Wilkinson, a Victoria retiree, told the novelist and magazine writer Howard O'Hagan that when he went to work for the Dominion Express in 1912, Wilson was already there. Then, wrote O'Hagan, he was "a man about thirty, a mere five foot six in height, slim, sallow and dapper, with a receding chin and large adam's apple, who often wore a red rosebud in his dark lapel." Those who encountered the young Wilson, said Wilkinson, "noticed his eyes, their irises so pale they faded in the whites."

Wilkinson also recalls that Wilson was a "smooth talker" who claimed he "was the son of an Anglican missionary and an East Indian princess and that he had served his time as an apprentice in a British navy windjammer."

Sometime before World War I, XII left Victoria and, predictably, left still owing the trusting Peggy Reynolds his back rent. His parting attempt at easing her mind was a promise that he would return, in Pierre Berton's words, "as the head of a new religion."

In 1941 Morton L. Bennett, the first person to write about Wilson for a magazine audience and a writer who interviewed many people who had known Brother XII, provides one last glimpse of young Wilson: "He left Victoria aboard a ship bound for the Orient."

Here our knowledge concerning Edward Arthur Wilson's Victoria years stood until 1967. That year, the prestigious U.S.-based publishing firm of Simon & Schuster of Canada Ltd. brought out *Canada's False Prophet*. The author of this biography of Brother XII was Herbert Emmerson Wilson, Baptist minister, veteran of the Boer War "where he befriended Winston Churchill"--and brother of Edward Arthur Wilson. The record could finally be straightened out.

Edward Arthur Wilson was born in Wyoming, Ontario, Herbert Wilson announced; his parents were Malcolm and Christina Wilson, firm believers in the gospel according to the King James Version, and every bit as strict as their beliefs could make them.

Wilson's childhood came to an abrupt end one summer night in 1886. That's when he ran away from home, minutes ahead of the arrival of an irate father--the father of a girl who was to bear the fifteen-year-old's child. Wilson's strict parents never again mentioned Edward Arthur's name within the hearing of his younger brother.

Early in the 1890s Herbert Wilson visited his older brother at an unspecified location, probably New Orleans. Edward Arthur was earning his way as "Swami Siva" who "knows your Past and your Future." Wilson was also associating with groups ranging from the theosophical and evangelical to the occult and magical. After this encounter between the brothers, Edward Arthur departed for the South Seas to study magic and sexual rites.

By 1898 he was back in Canada, this time in Calgary, where he was employed as a baggage clerk for the Dominion Express Company. During a trip to his "beloved Vancouver Island," Edward Arthur experienced his first recorded vision. "He was struck by a blinding light," according to Herbert Wilson. "He looked around him, and saw all the trees on fire, although none of them burned."

Herbert added another piece to the puzzle. "As usual [and this seems the only constant in Wilson's life during this period], the rugged beauty and serenity of Vancouver Island was one of his favorite subjects. He loved to talk about its woods, its lakes, and its wild game. He had always felt that his ultimate destiny would take place on Vancouver Island." No doubt his memories of his sailing trips up and down the island's east coast were among the few positive and happy things he could look back upon with any pride.

Finally, and after a great deal of persuasion from his brother, Edward Arthur spoke out about his thoughts. "The central root is unity," he said. "Mankind has allowed itself to be divided by great chasms of trivial misunderstanding into many religions. And so, religion has lost its meaning. And so, man has lost his security. Look around you, look at the isolated, the unhappy, the lonely! This, Herbie, is the result of lack of unity, this truly is the curse of the tower, the original sin. This is Every Man and One Man, doomed to eternal aloneness among crowds."

One can easily imagine how riveting all of this was for the younger man, who, it is obvious by his tone, worshipped his older brother. Put the two men in a boardinghouse room, add a series of evenings-after-work, give them the soft light of a kerosene lamp while outside the winter winds howl. Before this, visions, and the strength visions give, had only been glimpsed in the Wilson family Bible. No wonder Herbert Wilson remembered his brother's words so clearly many decades later.

Edward Arthur, a womanizer since puberty, announced to his brother that he had learned to live without women. Sex was a thing of the past in his life. No sooner had he made this decision than he made another: "He must leave enough offsprings to promulgate his religion."

III

Prophecy of Hope

The northwest Italian coast city of Genoa in the mid-1920s is the next link in the chain of places and events that would lead Edward Arthur Wilson back to his well-loved Vancouver Island. Either by design or happenstance, Genoa had become a global meeting place, a catalyst and a ground for those who sought answers in the spiritual sphere.

Astrologists, occultists and theosophists of various orders and persuasions gathered into little colonies of mutual interest, their doctrines ranging from the studious inclinations of the theosophists-- who believed in the spiritual nature of all matter and in improving the soul through reincarnation after reincarnation--to the more sinister practices of witchcraft. Of the latter, the most prominent of the demon-worshippers in Italy during the 1920s was Aleister Crowley.

Crowley called himself "The Great Beast" (the men and women who knew him called him much worse) and he practised the most degrading and degenerate forms of magic. Unlike the stage magician who creates illusions to deceive and entertain his audience, Crowley concentrated on the revival of ancient forms of sorcery. His aim was domination, and then the satisfaction of his bestial appetites.

Wilson was part of this mileu. We know from his own writings that he was on the French Riviera in October 1924 where, he told a friend, he was staying at a "very small place in the south of France, and quite alone." "In September 1925," he continued, "being ill and with very little money, I went to a small place in Italy where I could live cheaply and very quietly for the winter."

As Brother XII, Wilson would later tell the world about these months of suffering in *Early Letters*. During this period the messiah received from "The Master" the material that became his first book, *The Three Truths*, which a year later would propel him into prominence.

In Wilson's words, here is the incident of the Tau, Greek letter of the alphabet and occult symbol. "About 9:30 p.m., October 19, 1924, I was not well and had gone to bed early," he wrote. "At this time, I wanted to get some milk to drink, so lighted the candle which stood on a small table at the side of my bed. Immediately after lighting it, I saw the Tau suspended in mid-air just beyond the end of my bed and at a height of eight or nine feet. I thought, that is strange, it must be some curious impression upon the retina of the eye which I got by lighting the candle. I closed my eyes at once, and there was nothing there. I opened them and saw the Tau in the same place, but much more distinctly; it was like soft golden fire, and it glowed with a beautiful radiance. This time, in addition to the Tau, there was a five-pointed star very slightly below it and a little to the right. Again I closed my eyes and there was nothing on the retina. Again I opened them and the Vision was still there, but now it seemed to radiate fire. I watched it for some time, then it gradually dimmed and faded slowly from my sight.

"The next day I made a note of the matter," he continued, "and recorded my own understanding of it, which was as follows: 'The Tau confirmed the knowledge of the special path along which I travelled to initiation, i.e., the Egyptian tradition and the Star of Adeptship towards which I have to strive.' Now, today, the Master tells me that that is true but there was also another meaning, hidden from me then, but which he now gives us. The Tau represents the age-old mysteries of Egypt, and the Star of Egypt is about to rise; the mysteries are to be restored, and the preparation for that restoration has been given into our hands. In the great Cycle of the procession, the Pisces Age has ended, the sign of water and blood has set and AQUARIUS rises--the mighty triangle of Air is once more ascendant and we are to restore the 'Path of Wisdom and the First Path'-- knowledge."

About Wilson's experiences Pierre Berton observes: "At this point it is necessary to repeat that thousands of people came to believe implicitly in this gobbledygook, possibly because of Wilson's technique of presentation. The specifics of date and time, the confession of early doubt, the revelation that he was partially confused by the meaning of the symbols--these were the trappings of authenticity that lent a certain verisimilitude to the claim that he had been selected to undertake the restoration of the mysteries of Egypt."

Berton compares Wilson's descriptions to the writings of "that master of pulp fantasy, H.P. Lovecraft." Listen to Lovecraft: "A cold wind blew down that enormous aisle of pillars; somewhere in the endless distance lights seemed to move, then from above my head the light flooded me so that the distance and the vistas were dissolved. Then the light faded and I lay still, filled with a sense of wonder and great reverence....The Master bids me say that the voice was the Voice of Dhyanis, of the great Tutelary Deities of Egypt, whom, in the past, we worshipped as 'The Gods'."

The episode of the luminous vision led Wilson directly to composing *The Three Truths*. Beyond its contents, this book itself is valuable as a clue, for the cover shows us that as early as 1926 Wilson was using the name Brother XII. That early on, he set the name within quotation marks, and following it he has added "(the personal Chela of a Master)."

The book contains quite remarkable passages. "Hear ye the words I speak, and fear not," he admonishes, "for though destruction cometh upon many, yet for you it is the Day of Redemption. Ye shall come out of the House of Bondage, that House which is Egypt, which is even the body-consciousness."

His resonance heightens in his prose: "I am the Messenger of the Fire, the messenger of the Whirlwind, the Messenger of the day of Adjustment. The fire burneth but dross, that the silver and the gold may remain. By the Wind ye shall mount to the heavens--if ye be the children of discernment."

One newspaper man observed about his proclamations that "the number of such soul-swindlers is enormous, but for downright genius in the world of spiritual exploitation few can compare with Edward Arthur Wilson."

In *Early Letters*, Wilson explains how the next step in his life was dictated to him. "On May 15th," he writes, "Master told me to go to England to organize his Work there. You must understand that I was in poor health--in bed every day with heart trouble; I had no money beyond about five pounds over my actual railway fare, and I had no friends, for I knew not a soul in England who would have the least interest or sympathy with such a case." Wilson, Paul St. Pierre writes, "stepped back into the tangible world of places, names and dates in 1927 at Southampton, England. There he modestly revealed himself to be the Twelfth Master of Wisdom."

Alongside Wilson during most of this period was Alma, a woman of Scottish ancestry and well-educated; she was also Mrs. Wilson, everyone was told. She was with him in the Italian monastery where they were living when the other eleven brothers contacted him, and she would eventually travel with him and the Barleys to Vancouver Island.

Alfred and Annie Barley were the informants for writer Morton

Bennett when he described the furore Wilson was unexpectedly causing. "The theosophists of Southampton rallied around Brother Twelve like flies around a syrup pot," he wrote. "They spread his praises far and wide. He, and he alone, had completed the last of the Sacred White Circle. He was Brother Twelve. He was of them. The other eleven brothers had gone to their celestial rewards and were awaiting an earthly call from Brother Twelve. In order to get in touch with them he must go "sahmadi."

"Theosophists flocked from London and other leading cities," Bennett continued. "Awe-struck, they were led into the presence of the great Brother who was about to commune with the spirits on their behalf. The stage was set and Brother Twelve made the most of it. He slumped into a trance and for the better part of an hour uttered hideous moans and groans as he twisted and squirmed. Perspiration poured down his face. The spectators were impressed, then astounded, and from that point on Brother Twelve's influence was firmly established."

Alfred Barley was a retired chemical engineer and astronomer who had worked with the Greenwich Observatory. His wife Annie, also retired, had served for twenty-eight years as a teacher with the London County Council. In all haste they sold everything they owned--for only in that way could they afford to give Brother XII the money he demanded.

Another convert was Philip J. Fisher, son of the late Sir John Arbuthnot Fisher, a British admiral and the genius credited with sweeping reforms of the British navy during his time as First Sea Lord of the Admiralty. The young Fisher was rich, and Brother XII firmly advised a particular course of action. "You must change your worldly wealth into cash, bank notes or gold," Wilson told Fisher, "and bring it all to me. We will have little use for money where we are going."

In the 1930s Barley remembered Wilson then as a commanding figure, a man to be feared. When going into one of his trances, he said, "the strange mole on his cheek bobbed in rhythm with the convulsions of his wedge-like face."

The Barleys were present at one seance when the "other brothers" got word to Wilson to go samadhi-- into a trance. At once, while everyone was watching, he stepped behind a black curtain. About half an hour later he pulled the curtain aside. Of course there was "sweat on his forehead" and of course starlight glistened from the unplumbed depths of his eyes. When he spoke, Barley and the others learned that Wilson's masters had all been sitting around on a cloud looking down at a great bottomless void. Far far down, Wilson himself saw our world surrounded by our familiar galaxy.

Howard O'Hagan, writing in *Maclean's* in 1960, then as now one of Canada's best-known magazines, described what happened next. "The Sacred Brothers from their eminence had shown him where to build his 'place of refuge' on earth against the collision with Aquarius," O'Hagan wrote. "An assistant had unrolled an Admiralty chart against the blackboard and Brother 12 leveled his pointer against a spot off the west coast of North America--a spot he said he had never been to. There, he added, without blinking an eye, on an inlet on the eastern shore of Vancouver Island he would erect his 'fortress for the future'."

"It will be a wonderous land," Brother XII promised his excited listeners. "There we shall find a place by the sea. There will be trees around it, cedar trees. It will be our headquarters. We will create the Aquarian Foundation and it will usher in a new dispensation, a new sub-race to make way for the return of the 'Messenger'." The messenger's arrival time? "Somewhere around 1975."

Soon after this Brother XII booked passage for Montreal, and Alfred Barley handed him all the money he and his Annie could scrape together. It was a mere $14,000--a drop in the bucket compared to the money Brother XII would soon be banking--but it was his grubstake for a life in the new world.

IV

Cedar-by-the-Sea

A report in the *Daily Vancouver Province* described the miniscule Aquarian odyssey. "The little party crossed the Atlantic and the continent, stopping once or twice to confer with prospective members," the story runs, "but like a homing pigeon, Wilson led his little band of disciples directly to Nanaimo, and then five or six miles south on the old highway to Cedar and the island-studded waters near Boat Harbour."

In 1927, Bruce McKelvie's nationally syndicated column had a growing readership, and McKelvie had a nose for what his readers wanted. He began to take particular delight in providing his readers with progress reports concerning the Aquarian Foundation. "It was an excited little party," he reported, "that hurried back to Nanaimo [from Cedar] to start sending out telegrams and cables announcing the finding of the divinely appointed tract for the location of the Aquarian Foundation and the City of Refuge."

McKelvie described the response to Brother XII's colonial experiment as stupendous. The money, he said, began pouring in from every quarter: "One lawyer in Carthage, Missouri...would not wait for the slow-moving processes of the banks, or even for the mails to carry his donation. He wired $10,000."

By the summer of 1928, locals believed that as many as eight thousand members were making regular contributions. As Alfred Barley remembered, however, nobody was flush. "When we got there, no place had been provided," he said. "We were living in a furnished house, and had to build a place."

The people who formed the nucleus of the Aquarian Foundation were Alfred and Annie Barley, Wilson and his wife Alma, plus Frederick Pope and Captain Smith. Together they crowded themselves into a small house in Northfield, a settlement on the Esquimalt & Nanaimo Railway northwest of Nanaimo. It was there that Philip Fisher with his newly inherited wealth soon joined them.

Fisher's money provided the wherewithal to purchase a prime two-hundred-acre site, a location once the favourite meeting place of the Cowichan Indians. In the early summer of 1927, it was a peaceful and romantic spot dominated by first-growth cedar and fir. Fisher and the others began building what would soon become pleasant, sturdy homes.

Edward Arthur Wilson did not concern himself either with the selection of the colony's homesite or with the construction. He already knew the site his followers were bound to choose, so during this time he established the lucrative contacts that would be the basis of his princely fortune.

His attitude towards the property changed once the property deed had been recorded. He brought in a survey crew to stake out choice waterfront lots in the shape of the zodiac. These would be available, he told the other members of the Foundation, to those whom he would permit to live within the Inner Circle of the Aquarian Foundation.

At the apex of the Foundation's tract, shielded by huge trees and the soon-installed barrier wires, Wilson built his contemplation cottage, the sacrosanct Mystery House. No one but Brother XII was permitted entrance to this retreat.

These were golden days, island newspapers reported. Money was flowing in and the hotels at Nanaimo couldn't accommodate those who were driving up from California to sit at the feet of Brother XII.

One early donor, a man who would later join the Foundation, was Roger Painter, then known to many as the "Wholesale Poultry King of Florida." He did a yearly volume of nearly a million dollars, a very impressive sum in the 1920s. His contributions to the Aquarian Foundation were frequent and generous.

"Brother XII would write me for money," Painter later admitted candidly. "I would send him a cheque for $5,000 or $10,000 or more. I kept no accounting, but I do know when I gave my business to my brothers and came up here to dedicate my life to the work, I brought $90,000 in cash."

Others were joining the Foundation. Robert England was "a former United States Treasury agent." Will Levington Comfort was a writer with an international reputation. Sir Kenneth McKenzie came from England, as did A. Laker, a writer and editor. Maurice Von Platen, a millionaire whose wealth came from manufacturing pianos and organs, arrived from Chicago, and Joseph Brenner, a newspaper publisher, came from Ohio. The writer and scholar Coulson Turnbull found his way to Vancouver Island from Philadelphia, and James J. Lippincott, a member of the publishing family of that name, came from New York.

Something impressive was taking place at Cedar-by-the-Sea.

During the many study sessions interrupting the work on the land and property that first summer, Brother XII was called on repeatedly to explain to the newcomers why British Columbia had been chosen by the Brother XII's teachers.

"There are many reasons," he replied again and again, "not the least of which is the objective of body-building. In British Columbia the conditions are ideal for all-around personal development."

A writer of that period gives us another reason that made the island perfect. "The climate of Vancouver Island approximates closely to that of Great Britain," the report starts, "modified by the special circumstances of its geographical position. The proximity of the snow-capped Olympian mountains has a marked effect upon the summer temperature, which is never intensely hot, while the Japan current, striking the west coast, brings with it moisture and heat, which tempers the severity of the winter." The writer adds a few meticulous Fahrenheit specifics: "The yearly average temperature at Victoria is 48.84 degrees. Lowest average winter temperature 21 degrees, highest 57.4 degrees. The yearly rainfall averages 31.29 inches, snow 16.06 inches. Heavy snowfalls are exceptional and the snow disappears in a few days, sleigh drives being one of the rarest treats enjoyed by Victorians."

Even more important in Brother XII's scheme was the promise of vibrant longevity: "Unlike many mild climates, that of Vancouver Island is healthful, there is no malaria, no endemic disease, and the health department takes every possible precaution to prevent epidemics. Children thrive wonderfully in this favored land, and the aged and feeble find new life in its balmy, invigorating air."

There are few likelier places on Earth to spend time, should one desire to turn his or her back on the clamorous public world. Brother XII chose well.

It was, he also knew, a haven for believers and non-believers. Nearby Saltspring Island had been settled by former slaves from the United States in the 1850s and 1860s. No one had bothered the reclusive Danes who had colonized Cape Scott on the Island's northern tip in the 1890s. Even less interest had been shown in the socialistic Finns who chose to settle on Malcolm Island only a few miles further north of Cedar on Vancouver Island's east coast. In Victoria itself, Lily Adams Beck was writing two and three English-language bestsellers yearly and exciting no local interest whatsoever. Furthermore, Victoria or other communities on Vancouver

Island served as jumping-off spots to Britain's Asian empire or (and this was true for many) the first hideout to which some jumped when their "business" drew too much attention within that vast empire.

Why Brother XII chose that particular place is not hard to fathom. Cedar-by-the-Sea is the local name for a stretch of shore near Cedar, a post office and settlement described in 1892 (when Wilson first saw it) as being "about ten miles from the City of Nanaimo" and connected to that centre by a wagon road. It lay "in quite a farming section."

Fifteen years later, a gazetteer places it "seven miles south of Nanaimo." In 1919, a period during which almost all Vancouver Island settlements and villages began to describe themselves in tourism terms, Cedar was simply "a post office, farming and coal mining district, midway between Nanaimo and Ladysmith," and was connected to the Island Highway by an "auto road." Nanaimo's boundaries were now only six miles distant. Cedar had a school and an Anglican Church.

Cedar-by-the-Sea is not even mentioned in island travel literature of the period, and it doesn't appear on period maps. Small and isolated, the beautiful spot was the answer for members of the Aquarian Foundation craving to escape a rotten and godless world. A 1928 directory lists eighty-five persons resident in Cedar at that time. Most were farmers, miners or retirees, but there were exceptions: Mrs. T. Little was the storekeeper, her husband was the postmaster, Mary McMillan was a widow, G.G. Vincent was a schoolteacher and Miss M. Tolputt a domestic.

Although these elements made the area at the very least a good spot in which to avoid the contemporary world or, ultimately, the collision with the constellation Aquarius, Vancouver Island had another attraction. A sense of the place is offered by Negley Farson, airman, special correspondent, traveller and sportsman who lived at nearby Cowichan Lake only a few years before Brother XII's arrival at Nanaimo. "On our side of the lake," he wrote, "the whole twenty miles of shoreline held just two residents; a professional cougar hunter (and bootlegger)...and an old Irish doctor and his wife. Along this shore also lived a nomadic Englishman, honorary gamewarden, who moored his tiny houseboat wherever the whim moved him. And here I, too, securing one of these unpainted board shacks built upon a cedar raft, began a nomadic life that lasted two years."

Within a few miles of Farson lived a German exile in "a startling, red-painted 'schloss'," a trapper, an English aristocrat, a Scottish hermit. Then--empty miles until the logging camp. The loggers there "were Scandinavians, English 'remittance men,' Americans, even Sikhs. There were astonishingly few Canadians among them."

Brother XII knew this world well; he'd sailed up and down the east coast of Vancouver Island every summer during his years in Victoria. The Island was also a haven for rum-runners, opium-smugglers and many others who weren't in the habit of keeping office hours and didn't proffer receipts, but he knew a man could be himself in this atmosphere--and worship his own gods, in his own way, if he so wished.

Vancouver Island attracted off-beat religions--British Israelites, Kabalarians, Rosicrucians and Four Square Gospelers. Of these, "none [were] so kooky," wrote Pierre Berton, "none so bizarre, none so preposterous--none so downright evil--as the Aquarian Foundation, set up in 1927 on Vancouver Island by the man who called himself The Brother, XII."

Knowledge of Brother XII's nefarious plans lay in the future of those gathering at Cedar-by-the-Sea. A trail led to the clearing where the houses were being built, and just where the trail broke into the open was a great moss-draped maple. It soon became known as the Tree of Wisdom, for under it the guru held court. His disciples would gather at his feet to listen as their Master explained the philosophy for which he was the voice.

Nonresident Aquarians, the visitors and the mail-order converts, continued to flood into the small hostelries of Nanaimo, "the Hub City," then British Columbia's coal-mining capital. The locals were quick to figure out the Aquarians' routine, anticipating the disciples' early-morning exodus from Nanaimo to the acreage at Cedar where they spent their days visiting, teaching and studying, and, in turn, sitting under that magnificent old maple where they listened to their energetic teacher. Many of these visitors remained for weeks, so enamoured were they by the location and Brother XII's teachings.

As pleasant and sturdy homes rose to fill the landscape, most of the early shacks and makeshift shelters disappeared. Cedar-by-the-Sea was fast becoming an Aquarian Eden, distinguished by the reported absence of jealousies, bickering and normal conflict between neighbours. Men and women pondered the universe while their children played in harmony.

Everything was by plan, though few recognized the real outline. Brother XII was careful in his selection process. Only one man, or man and wife, from any specific geographical locality was chosen to remain among the elect in the Aquarian colony. In this way, those who responded to his invitation to remain were strangers to one another--reinforcing their dependency upon XII and his authority.

Other criteria applied, always suiting Brother XII's grand plan. The poor were as welcome as the rich. "Those who could not contribute their thousands," wrote one reporter, "could at least work." They were allowed to settle at Cedar-by-the-Sea and toil.

Increasingly, another factor began to attract Brother XII's attention--the daily mail. It became an irresistible lure. Each day Wilson seated himself at his counting table and opened each envelope slowly and carefully.

That done, he next set off (or sent his accountant, a job Robert England had taken) to one of the banks in Nanaimo or to one of the nearby towns, and converted the bank drafts to $20 gold pieces. A small amount of currency would occasionally be drawn, but only in amounts suited to fill the Foundation's immediate needs. The balance, and Brother XII was specific in the matter, was always collected in $20 gold pieces. Nothing else would do.

As everyone in Nanaimo by this time knew, he was a man of habit. From the first day he stepped out of his chauffered car in front of one of the many Nanaimo banks he patronized, Brother XII was never seen in anything but a conservative grey suit, with three handkerchiefs tucked away in various pockets. Black silk hose, highly polished black patent shoes and a faraway look contributed to his mystique. His vandyke beard was always neatly trimmed and his hair, the greyish tint hinting age and culture, was kept short. And he was strong, the towns' observers noted; he carried his canvas bags of Canadian $20 gold pieces as easily as though they were feathers.

V

Brother Mary and Isis

Grudgingly the forest gave way, a few feet at a time, to accommodate the gardens and pleasant homesites of the industrious colonists in those green summer months of 1927.

Autumn brought more than the usual seasonal changes. Brother XII's time in the Mystery House daily grew longer, and his disciples were no longer the centre of his attention, absorbed as he was in the silences inside that tree-hidden house. In there, he told his students, he and his ego ascended to higher planes for consultation with the Masters of Wisdom.

About this time Brother XII came up with a new task for the faithful. They were obliged to witness, but always at a discreet distance, their leader's frequent absences from his bodily form. Once his door closed, his flock was to line up along a wire that stretched across the pathway about a hundred yards from the Mystery House. Brother XII had instructed them as to what they must do.

"Concentrate! Meditate!" he'd ordered. "This will help me in the process of passing from plane to plane on my spiritual mission."

Participants never forgot how they gathered along the wire barricade, or the long periods of silence that accompanied such vigils. On occasion, when the quiet grew too heavy, one or another of the vigilants broke the spell to remark upon the weather or some other trivial matter--and then the silence fell upon their shoulders again.

Brother XII somehow knew of each infraction, no matter how slight. Everyone understood without question how he gained the information: it was obviously another sign of his power, for he was the one the Brothers of Wisdom had chosen. Next day, or even two or three days later, the angry Brother could be expected to storm from his clapboard retreat and "with eyes of cold fire" confront the hapless disciples. His knowledge of even their most minor indiscretions, even their innermost thoughts, kept the awed followers off balance. The faithful learned they could not keep secrets from their teacher.

Did Brother XII really have such psychic powers?

To this question came one answer from an electrician who hailed from Spokane, Washington. Early in 1928, the tradesman was on a bus bound from Vancouver back to Spokane when he struck up a conversation with a fellow professional, a mechanic with the British Columbia Electric Railway Company. The electrician remarked on a strange job he had just completed up near Nanaimo; he had installed nothing less than the finest microphone system west of the Rockies, he told his travelling companion.

"This was," the electrician boasted, "work I had to do in secret-- installing a number of microphones hidden behind foliage, stones and tree trunks along the line of a wire crossing a path, and leading to a mysterious cabin."

Electronic wizardry, not spiritual perception, was providing that black-hearted eavesdropper with the means to keep his flock submissive.

Other signs of Brother XII's curious behavior began to emerge. "A more friendly and sincere gentleman you couldn't possibly find," claimed Vancouver lawyer, Edward A. Lucas, one of the first Canadians to follow Brother XII. "It was not for about a year that he began to act strange. He predicted that the forthcoming presidential election in the U.S. would never be held; that there would be a general uprising and economical chaos, and he began to lay in supplies such as rifles, pistols and ammunition, also groceries."

It was at about this time--1927--that Edward Arthur Wilson, nicknamed "the skipper" by locals and known as Brother XII by thousands of followers, began using an even stranger array of names.

Edward Arthur Wilson adhered strictly to his nom de plume, Brother XII, in all matters relating to his calling but, in the secular world and especially in the banking communities surrounding Cedar, he was identified by any of several names. In Chemainus it was de Valdes, Amiel de Valdes. Other bankers knew him as Julian Churton Skottowe, but most welcomed the man making his weekly and sometimes daily rounds with cheques and money orders as plain old E.A. Wilson.

Some days it seemed that paper money was piling up faster than Brother XII could convert it into gold. He carried all the settlement's money, one banker remembered, in his own personal account. It was a substantial amount, with deposits often running into four figures, occasionally five. Shortly before the final trial in 1933, one banker said that someone, probably Wilson, had once deposited

$35,000 in one lump sum.

Brother XII daily preached his belief that Cedar-by-the-Sea provided the only sanctuary, the place of refuge, from the wrath of the Masters who were more determined than ever to eliminate all semblance of greed and evil from the surface of our planet. The possibility of his own greed did not ever come up for discussion.

The last person to see the gold Brother XII would tuck away at his refuge was not, as might be expected, Robert England, the Foundation's accountant. The last person other than Brother XII was a Mr. Coats, who because of his duties was privy to Brother XII's most important secret.

Coats was the Foundation's carpenter and, when called upon to do so by his leader, he built cedar boxes. Into these were fitted quart mason jars. Coats would then nail sturdy lids on each box when it was filled.

The mason jars were filled with money and then sealed with wax. Coats later claimed he'd built forty-three boxes for his lord and master. Each of these boxes, he continued, contained $10,000 in gold coin. Anyone can multiply forty-three by $10,000, but the sum doesn't total just $430,000. The sum adds up to an explanation as to why Brother XII remains so interesting. No one yet has found that hoard of nearly half-a-million, and it's not the sort of story that dies away with time.

Accountability for this influx of wealth was not part of Brother XII's game plan. He was certainly alert to the need for maintaining unchallenged authority among his followers and with those who enforced Canadian and British Columbian financial statutes. He expeditiously registered the Aquarian Foundation under the Societies Act as a non-profit religious order.

The colonists themselves did much of their business in the nearby village of Chemainus, frequently patronizing Stuart Clement's newly-opened drugstore. Clement reported that business with the Aquarians was brisk; they bought a year's supply of necessities at a time, whether soap or baby food. Other businessmen noted that the newcomers were often exacting, though fair, in their requirements.

One reporter later observed: "When J.L. Goldsmith's father helped one of them move his belongings, his possessions included more than $4,000 worth of food supplies--which, even at today's prices, is a lot of groceries."

Sometime during the winter of 1927-28, Brother XII received a note and cheque from Mary W.T. Connally. It had been forwarded to him via astrologer, lecturer and writer Coulson Turnbull. Pierre Berton describes the note as "a fan letter" that suggested "there was more [money] where that came from." Connally was the widow of a millionaire. She lived in Ashville, North Carolina, and though some have seen her as a half-tragic, half-comic figure, time proved she was no fool.

Brother XII, wrote Paul St. Pierre, "couldn't bear procrastination where money was concerned. He cabled Mrs. Connally to meet him in Toronto and [then he] hopped the Union Pacific train at Seattle." It was the most important train trip of Brother XII's career.

On the train, Edward Arthur Wilson quickly judged that Myrtle Baumgartner was certainly the most comely and compelling woman aboard. He promptly went about learning all he could about her. Myrtle was returning home to her husband, Dr. Edwin A. Baumgartner, a prominent physician at Clifton Springs, New York. For several weeks she had been on one of her frequent and extended western excursions.

No woman could long resist Brother XII's powers. Within hours of meeting the man she was in his private compartment; before she had cottoned onto what was happening, her clothes were off and she was in his bed. Years in the Orient had taught him more than one type of magic, and Myrtle's body responded to XII's hands and tongue in ways she would have believed impossible hours earlier.

They spent three days on the train together; by the time Wilson got off in Chicago, his travelling companion knew she must rush home, pack her belongings, say goodbye to her children and rush back to Wilson's embrace. Wilson meanwhile, back in his guise as Brother XII, continued from Chicago to Toronto and his appointed meeting with Mary Connally.

"We had a talk for about three hours," she'd later tell a packed Nanaimo courtroom. "He told me about the settlement, and we discussed the City of Refuge. One of the principal things I was interested in was the fact that children were to be in it, in the work."

We have this place for the children, Brother XII told her, but first we need the wharves, the houses and, most of all, the funds required for construction of the school, a magnificent structure to be named Greystones, with walls fully five feet thick.

"He had it in a nutshell," Mary Connally exclaimed to an amazed audience in 1933, "[and] I was convinced that was the work...which I was going to do in this world....He was to be the contractor as well as the architect."

At the conclusion of the meeting Mary Connally handed over a cheque for $25,580 to the delighted Brother XII. Mary Connally, now renamed Brother Mary, hurried off to North Carolina to finalize her plans for transferring her headquarters to Cedar, British Columbia.

Just as hurriedly, Brother XII shucked his religious trappings and caught a cab for the railroad depot and his rendezvous with destiny.

Back aboard the westward-bound train with Myrtle again ensconced in bed beside him, Wilson confided a galactic secret. "You are the incarnation of Isis, my historical counterpart. And I, Edward Arthur Wilson, am Osiris the sun god."

Next he showed her the cheque; being a god was good business. She was smart enough to realize that pretty fast. In their exuberance, or in the happiness at the ending of their long separation, Isis and Osiris (so he later confided to a friend) took the "Sixth Initiation."

Back home on the quiet shoreline of Cedar-by-the-Sea, a strange and uneasy peace had settled on the Aquarian Foundation. Roger Painter had been left in charge and he had proved to be a quiet and effective leader. Everyone would remember this period as the lull before the proverbial storm, but whatever work of a positive nature Painter's leadership accomplished was soon undone by the arrival of Isis and her brother-husband.

Stunned silence greeted the pair as they stepped out of the car in front of the Aquarian Foundation headquarters. This esoteric female was neither in the plan nor the script of established Aquarian prophecy. No flower petals were strewn before them as they made their way to the supremely private Mystery House, nor were the moralistic disciples prepared for their leader's revelation that he, Osiris, had at last been joined by his sister-wife, Isis.

"Does he think we're damn fools?" The reaction was shock and anger from the first. Brother XII's protestations that Isis was a virgin convinced no one-- particularly his wife.

There were angry mutterings, but none dared challenge the newly proclaimed sun god openly. As soon as the god and his lovely Myrtle goddess closed the door of the Mystery House, however, his disciples clustered around the still-undiscovered sound system to voice their outrage in no uncertain terms.

At this point Alma Wilson stood up at a meeting and denounced her husband. The rest could do what they wanted, but she intended to return home. So she did, too, and her parents paid her fare.

Realizing something tactical must be played out, and fast, Wilson went into a trance--to gain, he said, spiritual guidance from the Eleven Masters. No one was overly surprised when he returned with a strange verdict favourable to himself.

"The Masters of Wisdom," he claimed, "revealed disloyalty in the colony." In fact, said the Brother, it was only his pleadings that had prevented the spirits of the higher plane from "spreading the traitors over the rocks like so much butter." And Isis, he went on to say, was "destined to give birth to a child named Horus and Horus was to become, circa 1975, a second Christ."

This appeased no one. Brother XII next announced his plan to create another Aquarian settlement, this one to be called Mandieh. The truly elect at Mandieh would in turn join the holy brother-sister unity. To this end, he took $13,000 of the money contributed by Brother Mary in Toronto and purchased four hundred acres of prime land on Valdes Island. In that island's original house built by Captain William Flewett, god and goddess went into extended retreat.

The long-awaited news finally reached the dissidents at the Aquarian Foundation's headquarters at Cedar-by-the-Sea: a child had been born. The news that Horus had arrived drew the unhappy colonists together. Christ had returned. But the joy and hope for the future departed even faster than it had arrived. Horus, the boy god, was a girl.

VI

The Law and Osiris

"This is your punishment for your doubts," screamed Brother XII at his brethren after the birth of his daughter. "The Lord will take Isis away from us now. But he will send another, and may heaven help you if you doubt her."

On hearing she'd given birth to a girl, Isis (once more simply Myrtle Baumgartner) went insane, and XII, showing his true colours, ditched her as quickly as possible. The sex-starved deity now indulged himself with repeated visits to Vancouver, to meet secretly and frequently with various attractive and wealthy women. His spiritual powers continued to be as powerful as his sexual.

"You'll know me," he told them, "for I'll be wearing a red carnation."

Patience and faith are sturdy virtues but they're not indestructible. The endurance of the cultists, now never far from the breaking point, was being tested again. A newspaper article reported that the Aquarians were upset both with his trips to Vancouver and the resulting publicity, so to appease his followers as well as to gain spiritual guidance, Brother XII retreated to the Mystery House for seven days of profound meditation. The ever-gullible loyalists took turns standing the accustomed vigil along the length of wire that separated the secular from the spiritual at Cedar-by-the-Sea.

One morning the vigilants heard noises in the underbrush surrounding the Mystery House. Listening, they decided the noise was being caused by some farmer's dogs. Wanting no trouble, and not wanting their meditating leader to be disturbed, they waded into the bush to drive the dogs away. What the shocked guardians discovered was none other than Brother XII returning from a most earthly mission--as advertised by the rumpled red carnation in his lapel.

On top of this came another blow. This time it struck the most loyal of Brother XII's followers, the Barleys. A curt and abusive letter from Brother XII arrived at their home, accusing the pair of communicating with enemies and taking part in a variety of scandalous proceedings.

The motive behind this soon became apparent. They had moved into a pleasant new home only a few weeks prior to this unexpected letter's arrival. Robert de Luce of Los Angeles had about that time written of his interest in joining the Aquarian Foundation at Cedar. He had money and he needed a home. Was Brother XII the sort of fellow who'd turn this beseeching man away from his door? Now that Brother XII had bilked the hapless Barleys for all that they had in way of cash, all they had left to give him was their home. It would suit de Luce perfectly, he decided.

The problem was, for the Barleys and for many of the others, that Brother XII involved himself in every aspect of the Foundation's business. His control extended as well into the private lives of the Foundation's members. He missed nothing.

Intimidation was another tool he used with consummate mastery. Frequent assemblies had long been a part of Aquarian ceremony and daily routine. These assemblies were usually held at night, the perfect time for XII to add a touch of mystery, or one more element to confuse his followers. That knowledge is power was not an adage wasted on Brother XII.

One young disciple remembered something of Brother XII's method: "He made me an acolyte...I thought it was great stuff. He told me to strip needles from evergreen branches and dry them thoroughly. I was to fill the pockets of my robe with these dry needles and watch for his signal.

"He liked to invoke the spirits in outdoor sessions while standing over a small fire built on a stone altar. When he tipped me the signal, I would throw a handful of dry needles into the fire. The fire would flare up nicely and, hey, presto, there he was, all lit up, with his arms outstretched and looking like God."

Since the sordid episode with Myrtle/Isis, Brother XII's grip on his followers had been slipping. One man finally began to see room to manoeuver; this was Robert England, the once-upon-a-time secret service agent. As the Foundation's treasurer and head bookkeeper, he had made a discovery that sparked a revolution.

During one of Brother XII's trips to Vancouver, England had done a quick audit of the Aquarian Foundation's books. And it had to be quick: England had a healthy regard for the automatic pistol Brother XII carried at all times. But it didn't take England long to find where Brother XII had been dipping his hand into the till.

He immediately went to Nanaimo and charged Brother XII with stealing more than $5,000. England specifically pointed out Mary

Connally's large donations.

For dramatic detail few things written about Brother XII can compare with Morton Bennett's 1941 account. "Blissfully ignorant of these proceedings," Bennett wrote, "Brother Twelve was enjoying the balmy sea air aboard the *Princess Elaine.* He loved the sea, loved its mysteries. He felt it calling to him. Something else was calling, too, for when he stepped ashore in Vancouver he was greeted by policemen who placed him under arrest and sent him back to Nanaimo."

Gwen Cash, sometimes described as Canada's first woman reporter, described Brother XII at this time as a person who "hypnotized women, seduced them in a small house built deep in the forest, and signed cheques the board of Governors [of the Aquarian Foundation] hadn't authorized."

T.W. Paterson, an often-quoted and widely published western historian, reveals that at this time Brother XII was "enforcing slave labour and starving several followers no longer useful to him." More details steadily emerged concerning Brother XII's rampant misuse of the people and property of the Aquarian Foundation.

It is a wonder then that the increasingly inglorious Master found someone still with the faith in him to put up bail, but he did: "a gentle little woman who spoke with a soft, southern accent." With her by his side, Brother XII made his way to Aquarian headquarters. By this time Robert England realized that he had a tiger by the tail; with little adieu he headed for Vancouver. Until this case made it into court, he wanted to be out of reach of Brother XII's magic.

He was not fast enough. As he stepped down the gangway of the *Princess Elaine,* Robert England was arrested by the same policemen who had arrested Brother XII. And for the same charge--theft.

Briefly, this is what had happened: the British Columbia Provincial Police arrested Brother XII and brought him back to Nanaimo. There he counter-charged Robert England, claiming his accountant had embezzled $2,800 from the Aquarian Foundation's account. When arrested, England claimed this money represented back wages, but Brother XII refused to withdraw his charges, saying that the Foundation paid no salaries.

The preliminary hearing began on an unnaturally warm day in September 1928. No one was comfortable. The night before, Gwen Cash and Edward Lucas had had supper with Robert England, and later that night he disappeared. Most thought he was murdered by Brother XII's henchmen as he crossed the Strait of Georgia aboard the *Princess Elaine.* Everyone at the opening day of the trial guessed that Robert England would not appear. Only Brother XII knew with certainty what we all know today: England would never be seen again.

"Never," wrote Gwen Cash, "had the little courthouse in Nanaimo seen wilder scenes. They were like something out of the witchcraft-believing Middle Ages. Witnesses went into the box clutching magic stones to protect them[selves] from Brother Twelve's evil eye. One witness was carted off to a mental hospital. Another fell down in a faint when Brother Twelve glared at him."

This was the case that Chief Justice Aulay MacAulay Morrison would later call "the strangest ever to come before a Canadian court."

With an eye for telling detail, newspaperman Paul St. Pierre in the early 1950s wrote about that 1928 court scene: "Frank Cunliffe, a Nanaimo barrister with a keen eye for a tort but scarcely one to be accused of celebrating the Black Mass," he wrote, "apparently unleashed the first spiritual shaft. As counsel for Brother Twelve, he was cross-examining James Janey Lippincott (of the publishing Lippincotts) on the witness stand. Lippincott mentioned that a fellow disillusionist, one Coulson Turnbull, Ph.D., was in the court.

"'Indeed,' said Mr. Cunliffe, 'I shall have pleasure in asking many questions of Mr. Turnbull.'

"A low moan from the rear of the courtroom announced that the professor had fainted. Two or three others toppled over in sympathy. Court adjourned while air and ammonia salts were applied."

"The trial before magistrate C.H. Beevor-Potts," wrote Gwen Cash, "lasted most of two months." Yet, so sure of his case was defence lawyer Frank Cunliffe that he felt it necessary to call only one witness--Mary Connally. Morton Bennett was thinking of Mary's planned appearance when he wrote, concerning England and his cohorts: "Their plans, however, hadn't taken Brother Twelve's first, second and third lines of defence in consideration. Nor had they considered his reserves. Though they didn't know it at the time, they were going into this battle of wits without a feather to fly with. But not Brother Twelve. He had the feathers, the birds, and the nest too."

When asked a question by England's lawyer, the old-fashioned T.P. Morton, Mary Connally interrupted him: "I beg your pardon," she said with quiet dignity. "Brother Twelve has a perfect right to spend that money as he chooses. I gave it to him as a personal gift. It has nothing to do with the Foundation funds."

The magistrate gasped, as well he might.

"You gave him twenty-five thousand dollars as a gift?"

"Twenty-five thousand eight hundred and fifty," the little lady corrected. "I have here a marked cheque for twenty-eight thousand dollars. I wish you to see me give it to him as his own personal funds. I don't want any more misunderstandings about my gifts to Brother Twelve. Here, take this cheque. It is yours to do with as you wish."

There wasn't much to say after that genteel tour de force. England's supporters had had the rug pulled out from under them. There was still one more surprise left, though, one of those moments that live on in history with a life of its own.

During his flowing summation of the Crown's case against Brother XII, plaintiff's counsel Morton suddenly stopped "mid-way in his address, in mid-sentence." Then followed "an embarrassed shuffling of feet." Finally, Morton leaned over to Frank Cunliffe to admit, "This is ridiculous, but I've forgotten what I was saying."

Forget? An experienced lawyer such as Morton was does not "forget." The Aquarians were sure they knew the truth. Not one of them in the Nanaimo courtroom doubted but that it had been the result of Brother XII's black Egyptian magic.

This odd little episode was the end of the trial. Magistrate Beevor-Potts passed the case to assizes. The jury returned a verdict--no case.

After denouncing the traitors around him, Brother XII soon began developing new property on De Courcy Island, one of the De Courcy Group between Cedar-by-the-Sea and Valdes Island. It was bought with further monies supplied by the faithful Brother Mary, according to Howard O'Hagan, who did his own research in the area in the 1960s. On one of the islands the disciples of Brother XII began building new homes--being allowed to build there was apparently a sign of Brother XII's trust in that person. He bought a sawmill, built a school, and purchased "an ocean-going tug, which he re-named *Kheunaten*."

While the faithful cleared their land with their own strength and hand tools, Brother XII bought a tractor to use in his own land-clearing projects. According to later memories, these people worked daylight to dark. In the cool of the night, the tired workers would all gather to hear one of Brother XII's inspirational talks.

"The hour has struck," he might say, "for this earth to be plowed and harrowed. I have been called to drive the plow. You must choose whether you will be the plowshare or the clod which is broken, for the ground must be prepared that the seed may be sown."

Sometime during this period, Brother XII awoke from one of his trances to announce the pending arrival of a "High Priestess." This woman "would come from a place called Florida. She would have control over all the women members." The members braced themselves, and waited.

VII

Madame Zura

During this period on De Courcy Island, Gwen Cash has written, Brother XII "built storehouses, and erected fortifications, yoked women like oxen to ploughs, and adopted a new name, Julian Churton Skottowe. This name he borrowed from his latest mistress, a woman with a sharp tongue and an authoritative manner, whom he called Madame Zee."

Cecil Clark, a sergeant with the British Columbia Provincial Police when he visited the De Courcy settlement in 1933, and later a local historian of some note, remembered that Brother XII "bought a small sawmill, cut timber and built houses, including a giant store house for canned and bottled vegetables and fruit. A school house was built, complete with blackboards and desks, and a teacher imported from Switzerland."

Of the faithful but unlucky Mary Connally, Clark added: "Mrs. Connally was scheduled to have a nice house out of the deal. But Wilson [Brother XII] ratted out on this, and ended up by selling her a shack at Cedar for $5,000, which he bought for $1,500! And told her she wasn't to set foot on De Courcy Island, bought with her money!"

Pierre Berton was quite right when he maintained that to this point, "the tale of The Brother XII has been merely bizarre. With the arrival of the unspeakable Madame Zee, it becomes grotesque."

When Roger Painter arrived from Florida with $90,000 in his suitcase, his companion was Mabel Skottowe. She has been described as in "her thirties...tall, red-headed, so thinlipped that her mouth was no more than a horizontal scar."

Brother XII experienced another reincarnation right about then and began calling himself Amiel de Valdes.

Mabel was no Isis, not even another Alma Wilson. While renaming Madame Zura at a very elaborate ceremony, Wilson/Amiel de Valdes informed his disciples of her organizational status. "She is my eyes, my mouth, my ears," he told them. "And what she says you can take as coming from me." The listeners soon learned that Madame Zura was quick-tempered and never forgot a slight; her foul tongue "scourged like a lash." Whenever her words could not force the disciples into obedience and silence, she took to carrying a bull whip. No one argued with her after one taste of snapping leather.

"The members didn't rebel against her harsh rule," Morton Bennett commented. "They said she was a mistress of the devil and had been sent to test Brother Twelve. They were right. She was certainly a devil, and one without a saving grace. Of beauty she had none. Tall, angular, with blazing black eyes...[her] thin features were hard, her lips were like lines across her cruel face."

Described by some writers as a "complete sadist," Zee reserved her worst treatment for Mary Connally. One night Zee and a gang of followers rousted the elderly and unwell Mrs. Connally from her bed and informed her she was being moved to Valdes Island. She was given an island shack to live in, and to feed its heater-of-sorts Mrs. Connally was forced either to burn her furniture in it or stumble along the beach seeking driftwood. Leona Painter, Roger Painter's wife, was given the job of harassing the older woman and did a good job. Mary Connally was repeatedly forced to move her belongings from one shack after another, each more tumbledown than the last.

If it can be imagined, the plight of Mrs. Georgina Crawford was worse. She and her husband, Bruce, were from Lakeland, Florida. Young, petite and extremely good-looking, she was first put to work grubbing stumps by hand. When her exertions proved useless, she was made a goatherd and forced to work from before dawn to after sunset. One day she injured her knee badly in a fall. Instead of allowing time for the knee to heal, Madame Zura drove Georgina Crawford sharply back to work.

She fell and injured the knee once more. Useless as a goatherd, she was led stumbling and falling to "a warehouse full of hundred-pound sacks of potatoes and told to lift them down one at a time, spread out the potatoes, pick out the rotten ones, and re-bag the rest." As her knee gave her no physical freedom to manoeuver the bags, young Mrs. Crawford proved helpless at this task --but this was not the end of her torment.

"You're unfit to work among us," stormed Madame Zura, who then banished the browbeaten woman to the far end of the island. Later, once the knee healed, Madame Zura gave her the task of painting a shack. Three of its walls were easily reached, but the fourth hung over the edge of a cliff. Below it there was a thirty-foot drop to the sea. If she did not paint this wall, she was told, she would be forcibly separated from the one person she knew she could still trust --her husband. Physically and psychologically, Georgina Crawford was broken.

"Black Friday" and the stock market's crash late in 1929, as more than one author has noted, put the fear of the Lord into XII, but he knew gold would survive whatever would happen. The market crash, plus the troubles then breaking out daily in Asia and the breadlines and riots of the Depression--all seemed to substantiate what Brother XII had long been preaching to his nightly assemblies of followers. Armageddon wasn't far off.

The money continued to pour in, and as it arrived Brother XII turned the paper into gold in a version of the Midas touch, updated. The gold standard was one thing Brother XII believed in whole-heartedly.

Word of mouth throughout the vast and well-established net-work of theosophists was how Brother XII first reached the men and women who would become paying members of his Foundation. While discussion within theosophical circles continued to bring people into the fold, another and more effective method had been found to reach potential members once the Foundation was located at Cedar-by-the-Sea--a small magazine called *The Chalice*.

One of the few writers to have read Brother XII's magazine describes it as a "curious monthly, subtitled 'The Herald of the New Age,' [which was] crammed with much pure nonsense; among other items, it included some unsavoury ravings against the Jews, the Jesuits and the Bolsheviks, unlikely bedfellows who were seen to be co-operating to secure world domination--a suspicion commonly held by members of the fanatic fringes of that time on both sides of the Atlantic."

The Chalice was what first had attracted Mary Connally to the Aquarian Foundation. Although Brother XII is credited with writing and editing this journal, he had an unusually good backup staff. Will Levington Comfort was a writer, today best known for his work in the old *Saturday Evening Post;* Mr. A. Laker was the editor of a British-based magazine called *The Referee;* Joseph Brenner was the publisher of *The Sun,* a newspaper in Akron, Ohio; a member of the Lippincott publishing family was there, too, as was George Hubbard, identified as a Toronto newsman. Coulson Turnbull was the author of various books and magazines, as was Brother XII himself. Little wonder *The Chalice* proved so effective.

The compact $20 Canadian gold pieces continued serving as the common denominator of Brother XII's growing wealth, it was said. Money poured in with each day's mail, but no one was ever allowed to watch him opening the envelopes. Brother XII was not about to make the same mistake he'd made when he gave Robert England free access to the ledgers. Even more money was handed over when visitors arrived or departed.

Outwardly, nothing could have been more peaceful than the Aquarian Foundation's new settlement on De Courcy. Back at Cedar-by-the-Sea, most of the dissidents of the 1928 rebellion had either decamped (Edward Lucas, for instance, who had returned to his lucrative Vancouver law practice) or had made amends with Brother XII.

In this seemingly idyllic setting, security became an obsession with Brother XII. His concern grew daily for the safety of his fabled hoard of tidily boxed quart jars--jars that held $3,000 apiece in gold coins. More than once his furtive figure was seen carrying and secreting small heavy bundles carefully wrapped to disguise their identity.

Brother XII's routine was orderly and systematic. Off into the night he would tiptoe to one of his hideyholes to add his latest jar to the rapidly increasing collection. Mobility became as much a part of his obsession as did secrecy. He would frequently order a new hideaway dug; it would be left empty and uncovered, observed only by the chosen who were allowed to dig for their leader. Next morning, the holes were once again filled in.

Bruce Crawford, husband of the nearly martyred Georgina and captain of the colony's tugboat, was one who clearly saw and remembered the nervous movements of Brother XII. He was also directly involved with rotation of the cedar chests filled with the heavy and precious mason jars.

"He would bury it on one part of the island, and then a few days later he would dig it up again and take it to some other place. I was running the tug at that time," Crawford reported.

Others were involved as well. Alfred Barley contributed an anecdote to the growing collection of stories about the gold. As Madame Zura and Brother XII were preparing for an extended trip to England, he remembered Brother XII coming to his house one night carrying a burden wrapped in a towel.

"Take care of this," Brother XII commanded. "I am afraid of fire."

Barley was further instructed to continue the normal routine in his master's absence--to fill empty jars with coins, seal them with wax and bury them after each cedar chest was filled.

For his daily financial needs, Brother XII continued to rely on Mary Connally and other sources. When the Foundation's tug required a new engine, it was Mrs. Connally who immediately put up the cash. The gold stayed put.

Then several things happened that convinced Amiel and Zura de Valdes it was time to move on.

Early in 1929 after a series of disastrous lawsuits in New York City, Mary Connally lost her wealth. That put her point blank on Madame Zura's vindictive blacklist. Mary Connally was expendable, but without her open chequebook to milk at will, Brother XII knew he must replace his angel, and fast.

Then came the curious matter of the Ruddles. Brother XII might have survived his problems, but what it led to only underlined his vulnerability. Like his mortality, this was something he didn't care to see violated.

One of the clearest versions of the Ruddles story is the one told by former policeman Cecil Clark. "Carlin Ruddle and his young bride . . . spent their honeymoon powerboating in B.C. waters," Clark reported, "and in due course anchored in a De Courcy Island bay. They met Wilson, who turned on the charm. He didn't like Ruddle, but he liked what he saw of young Mrs. Ruddle. Privately he told her she should leave her husband and join the community. Believe it or not she returned to Seattle just long enough to pack a few things and disappear . . . ."

She reappeared at the De Courcy Mystery House. Guessing what had happened, her husband turned up shortly afterwards, having rowed there from Chemainus. Brother XII told him he was crazy, but all the while the man's new bride was hiding in the attic. Still shouting, Ruddle was put under armed guard overnight and in the morning was put into his rowboat and towed back to Chemainus.

Madame Zura, hardly stupid enough (or enamoured, as was her companion) to be blind to the trouble this affair might cause, ordered the girl to be rowed to some distant beach and kicked ashore. She was found some days later, starving and half-mad, by Japanese woodcutters.

While this was happening, Staff-Sergeant J. Russell, the officer in charge of the Nanaimo police district, was on his way to De Courcy with Mrs. Ruddle's distraught husband. Instead of wandering off or giving up, Ruddle had gone directly to the nearest police station. This suited the police just fine. They had long wanted an excuse to visit the island. The smouldering rumours were beginning to throw out sparks as the police had known they must, sooner or later.

Paying a call on Brother XII, they found him ready to admit, just as he had admitted to Mr. Ruddle, that the young woman had indeed been there but she had quickly left. He did not know where she had gone, he told them. No one believed him, but after searching all around De Courcy they had to believe she was no longer on that particular island. Of course she wasn't; by that time she was stumbling through the bush above some other distant saltwater beach.

Brother XII had money and a woman, and Europe waiting for him. After the awkwardness surrounding the scandal of the Ruddle couple, why remain any longer on De Courcy?

VIII

Hell on Earth

"Nobody could truthfully say that Amiel and Zura made a lovely couple as they set out on their holiday," Vancouver Island historian Harry Olsen once remarked, adding that the scrawny and awkward Zura stood inches taller than her swarthy escort and that her eyes held all the warmth of a pair of marbles. "As for Amiel, no one could guess that this ugly little man with the moth-eaten beard was actually the dynamic leader of a worldwide order."

Some people doubt that the trip was a holiday venture at all. Brother XII had lost the use of Mary Connally's money; this as well as the police visit may have been the reason for his overseas jaunt in January 1930. Finding new suckers, however, may not have been as easy as Brother XII imagined. Rich and poor alike in 1930 were tightening their belts.

To safeguard his investments, Brother XII transferred title of the original settlement of Cedar-by-the-Sea to the long-faithful and still-trustworthy Alfred Barley. Roger Painter, the one-time Florida chicken king, was appointed the colony's spriritual guide. "I call it the slack water period. You may call it whatever you choose to call it," Mary Connally later told the crowded courtroom at the final trial.

The prophet's infrequent letters from England revealed little but offered a proliferation of advice. He had met many well-wishers, he informed the people at home and, yes, he was picking up more donations to further the cause. The letters to Painter soon took on a certain tone, even while continuing to provide instructions, that convinced Painter something was terribly wrong with Brother XII.

One letter in particular addressed to Painter contained a detailed set of instructions in the matter of executing a number of people that Brother XII now obviously considered his prime enemies. The orders were terse and specific.

Painter was to kill by "etheric assassination" the following people: the Hon. R.G. Pooley, Attorney-General of British Columbia; the Hon. Joshua Hinchcliffe, Minister of Education; Edward A.

Lucas, Vancouver barrister; and Maurice and Alice Von Platen, the rich couple from the United States. The reasons behind these ordered assassinations are clear.

Pooley was the official who had cancelled the charter of the Aquarian Foundation. Lucas was an early supporter of the Foundation who had deserted Brother XII just days before the 1928 trial. The Von Platens had seen to it that their money was where Brother XII could never reach it. Why Hinchcliffe was on this hit list is not known.

The mechanics of the executions were to be those taught to Painter by Brother XII, a method by which he split his enemies' ethereal bodies from their physical bodies. Death in such cases appears to the authorities as having been caused by completely natural causes, Brother XII assured the nervous and unbelieving Painter in the letter.

Painter explained the procedure to the wide-eyed courtroom audience in 1933: "Now then, in arcanum work...people sit in a circle or triangle or in a shape in whatever form they elect to sit. The Brother...would always choose someone for whom he had an implacable hatred. He would stand them up in front of his imagination, and then he would begin his tirade, cursing and damning that spirit, then going up this way and down that way with his hands."

Roger Painter continued his nothing-but-the-truth account with graphic descriptions of "this most sinister" process, telling his listeners how Brother XII would describe a vertical stroke with his hand going from the head downward, then horizontally from left to right, cutting away the ethereal or finer body of the victim. Then, Painter said, Brother XII would cut away the spiritual body from which the physical body received its strength. "Then he would cut that, and the physical body's organism would finally become depleted and die. Such was the process of mental murder," he concluded.

The victims marked for soul-murder did not in fact perish as specified by Brother XII. Painter wanted none of it. Still, soon afterwards, Maurice Von Platen fell victim to a fatal bout with pneumonia on a trip home from Hawaii. His wife Alice soon followed. The diagnosis of her death was "intestinal stricture." In the course of time others on the death list succumbed to the more commonplace effects of stroke and heart attack. Curiously, one keeled over while preparing to make a dinner speech on the subject of "The Strange Personality of Brother XII."

Meanwhile, still suffering from the reverses of the New York lawsuit, Mary Connally returned home to North Carolina to defend herself in yet another legal action. Brother XII had not given up on her and her money supply completely, but he was no longer the gentle counsellor he had once been. His advice was downright painful to the elderly woman, who once so proudly had become Brother Mary.

When to her deep distress she lost this second trial, Brother XII wrote to her: "You are absolutely responsible for losing your lawsuit." Smarting under this criticism, Mary Connally insisted she had followed his instructions to the letter. In an earlier letter Brother XII had detailed for her a step-by-step courtroom strategy. It had failed and he was furious at losing the money that otherwise should have found its way into his hands. He ordered her to return immediately to his De Courcy stronghold in British Columbia.

Brother XII next wrote to the Barleys, who were by then in charge of the Foundation's business. They were to sell his own home in Cedar-by-the-Sea to Mary Connally, he told them. The selling price was to be $4,000, despite the fact that everyone including Mrs. Connally knew it was worth less than half that much. It was eventually revealed that this swindle was not so much for the money (which Brother XII welcomed nonetheless) but to keep the property out of the hands of Alma Wilson, his absent wife. He had once promised her the home as a peace-offering, and she seemed to be making ready to start a claim on it.

Another letter to the Barleys attested to Brother XII's excellent recall in certain matters. Remembering that the Barleys were about to come into an inheritance, and one of considerable size, Brother XII wrote with a beguiling suggestion. "Don't you think," he cajoled, "a nice thing to do with the money would be to put it into Greystones that we are about to build? You could have your apartments there and live with me in that building, and it would be a palatial mansion."

While still in England, Brother XII decided he needed a yacht, a good-sized vessel, and for this he needed another angel. He found one of each. He bought the *Lady Royal,* a trawler that had been rebuilt as a yacht with seagoing potential, and the money for his new find was supplied by a beaming benefactoress.

The vessel was almost new, having been launched in 1923 in Brixham, Devon. Cecil Clark saw the *Lady Royal* when she first arrived in British Columbia waters. "It's quite a curiosity, you know," he remarked, "because there are no more Brixton trawlers. And built, by God! They used timbers that lay for years under the shingled beach at Toro Bay, seasoning, pickling, you might say. Oak! And impossible to damage the damned thing."

Even Bruce McKelvie enthused about the Foundation's latest vessel: "She was a sweet little vessel to delight the heart of any sea-lover."

The *Lady Royal* had no auxiliary engine. The navigational feat of sailing it out from England to the west coast of North America, and then weaving through the tidal currents of the Gulf Islands proved, whatever else Brother XII might know, he knew ships and the sea. In Central America he had sent his white crew back to home port and had hired two Indians instead. With this new crew and the unflappable Madame Zura, Brother XII in due course dropped anchor off De Courcy Island.

Morton Bennett, writing less than ten years after Brother XII's return, described the clandestine arrival of the trawler. "The home-coming was quiet," he wrote. "The *Lady Royal* stole into harbour late at night without going through the formality of reporting at the Customs or Immigration [as required by law]. Several boxes were taken ashore under cover of darkness. These were hidden in the House of Mystery. Brother Twelve then reported to Immigration and blandly pointed out that two of his crew members were aliens and should be returned to Panama. The Indians were brought before the Immigration officials at once. Brother Twelve smiled. 'It has been a pleasure having you,' he said. 'I must give you some-thing to remember me by.' He turned to one of the Immigration officers. 'Lend me a dollar,' he said. The astonished official gave him a dollar bill wondering what he was going to do with it. The gracious Brother Twelve gave it to the Indians. 'There is something you will always cherish,' he said, and hurried away before anyone had time to recover from their surprise."

Were those smuggled boxes filled with rifles and grenades to begin fortifying his island stronghold, as Howard O'Hagan claimed? This seems a far more likely possibility than the rumoured opium. From an Edmonton mail order house Brother XII was ordering fourteen rifles and a thousand rounds of ammunition; a stone fort was being built on De Courcy and rifle-pits dug. Sentries walking guard duty day and night were ordered to shoot any boater who approached the shore.

No one was happy to see the Brother XII and Madame Zura arrive back at De Courcy from England. While they were away everything had gone smoothly, giving the colonists an idea of how truly good and productive their lives could be. Alfred Barley and

Roger Painter had worked well together, but with Brother XII back in residence the men and women dreaded what might be coming. Painter, since he had no "scalps" for Brother XII despite the soul-murder directives, was not looking forward to his first interrogation.

"Brother Twelve was now worse than ever," Morton Bennett wrote. "His temper was fearful. He and Madame Zura raged and stamped among the trembling folks who had given [them] their all. He put many of them to work careening his navy. He had two powerful boats now, both fit for ocean service, besides other small power craft."

The *Lady Royal* and the powerful *Kheunaten* were to be kept ready at all times for immediate use, he ordered. Brother XII knew that riflemen in the pits could hold off island-storming government policemen or soldiers long enough to allow himself and Madame Zura to escape. He appears to have convinced her that all this would work, because there is no record (as there had been earlier) of Zee trying to make Brother XII behave within the limits of the law.

He began to clean house. Mary Connally was ordered to leave but having no money and nowhere to go, she refused. William Lowell, a farmer or rancher from Nevada who had given the Foundation his last $3,000, was also ordered out.

Sarah Tuckett was seventy-six, a former schoolteacher and a cripple since childhood; she is said to have spent most of her time in the De Courcy Island cabin crying with pain and loneliness. "This afternoon," Brother XII told her one day, "a young man will take you for a row in the water." Surprised and pleased by this pleasantry, she began to thank Brother XII when he waved her into silence.

"While he rows, you sit way in the back seat and lean back, and back and back."

Miss Tuckett pointed out the obvious: "I'll fall in and drown."

"That's more or less correct," Brother XII admitted. "But don't you see? After you drown you will enter a high plane of existence."

Sarah Tuckett had long been convinced that when it came time for her to go to her Maker, on whatever plane he might exist, she would hear a voice calling. She didn't hear the voice as she was rowed around De Courcy Island, so she returned alive and dry. Ordered to go out again, she again landed safely, much to Brother XII's disgust. He brightened considerably when she promised to try a third time.

The next morning, minutes before the boatman was due to

arrive, a surprised Sarah was called upon to open her door. A noisy group of people crowded inside.

"Are you with us or against us?" shouted the crowd's spokesman. "Are you with us against Brother XII? He's gone back on us. He's no good. The Devil's got him. Here's our new leader, Roger Painter!"

She later admitted that she did not know what to do or say--but join them she did.

The final chapter had started. Exodus from De Courcy Island was the only next step.

IX

The Final Days

They held their breath in the crowded Nanaimo courtroom on the morning of April 2, 1933 as Mary Connally stepped into the witness box. Since her appearance in court in 1928, Lady Mary, as the locals respectfully referred to her, was thought to be the keystone to Brother XII's evil empire. Once she began speaking, everyone expected Brother XII to fall into the grave he'd dug for himself.

"The other day, your Lordship," she began in her soft-spoken manner, "I went over there [De Courcy Island] and found the place absolutely wrecked. You never saw such vandalism in your life. There is very little water on De Courcy, and the water tanks were shot through with bullets; windows smashed, trees felled on the houses; you cannot conceive of such things. The school room that they had fixed to house the children, they had taken the desks and chairs and smashed them out through the windows onto the ground, showing the spirit in which they were leaving, and the whole place has been left desolate."

"Who left it that way?" His Lordship asked.

"The defendants left it, and more than that; they sold the things that we had bought with the people's money. They sold four thousand jars of canned goods that these people worked day and night to put up."

Continuing with her detailed testimony, Mary Connally declared that she had written a cheque for $250 to pay for a horse and a stump-puller; $100 to buy fruit trees; $100 for goats; $45 to Alex Smith, a carpenter; $35 for tools needed by Mr. Lowell, and numerous smaller items for which she was asked to pick up the bill. Also, she remembered, she was asked for $1,500--or was it $2,000?--to pay Frank Cunliffe's fee for his defence work in the case brought by Robert England in 1928.

When it came time for Frank Cunliffe, again the defence lawyer, to stand up and begin his case, His Lordship Aulay MacAulay Morrison, Chief Justice of the Supreme Court of British Columbia, spoke sharply. "You have nothing to base your submission on," he boomed. "You didn't even bother to have your client here. You are his solicitor, and you shouldn't appear if you don't know where he is--having regard for what it is about and the whole form of the matter."

The whereabouts of the elusive defendant was later clarified by a former bellman at the Empress, Victoria's world-famous hotel. The bellman swore that Brother XII and his stony-faced companion were registered in that ivy-swathed hotel during the entire period of the emotionally charged trial. According to the same fellow, Madame Zura had ordered the latest edition of every newspaper delivered to their rooms so they could follow the day-by-day progress of the trial.

The judge continued his scolding: "I am surprised that any counsel would come here and, apparently, I suppose there must have been instructions from someone when this fabricated defence was put in?"

Frank Cunliffe was cornered but proceeded gamely. He was repeatedly cut off by Justice Morrison who, with a superbly confident Victor Harrison, the plaintiff's counsel, took turns heaping humiliation on the loyal but hapless Cunliffe.

The lengthy court transcripts reveal abundant examples of the colourful verbal exchanges that delighted the onlookers and filled reporters' notebooks:

"I thought you knew your defence, Mr. Cunliffe?

"But, but..."

"You can look up your defence at luncheon."

The baiting and scolding soon turned to outright insults from the bench.

"I don't want to hear any lies," Judge Morrison angrily admonished Cunliffe. "Embalm it with the other literature. You cannot make me hear it, thank you. I would rather read it myself than hear you read it. The one is a white lie, and the other is a yellow one."

The aroused judge then turned to Victor Harrison who, as the victim's attorney, had every reason to be confident.

"How much money are you wanting? You have got it your own way, and there is no defence. I will give you judgement now if I know how much I am to give. There will be an accounting of all monies taken from the plaintiffs. Do you want that? This is the time to ask for things, because I am in a mood to give them."

Chief Justice Morrison, Howard O'Hagan tells us, then "awarded Mrs. Connally $26,500 for money she had advanced, $10,000 damages and the four hundred acres on Valdes Island. Barley won his case for the return of $14,232."

It was a hollow victory, for all that. Brother XII and his consort were gone--gone, some said, on their ocean-going tug the *Kheunaten*, gone with their gold and their secrets.

To understand the layers of meaning of this so-called triumph, we must circle back to the day Sarah Tuckett and the others began their exodus from the De Courcy Island settlement.

As they made their way toward a boat they planned to steal for their trip to Vancouver Island and Nanaimo, where they wanted to file their complaints, the group most unexpectedly discovered Brother XII and Madame Zura leaving the House of Mystery. Both were wearing revolvers, both were carrying rifles, and between them they were manhandling a case of dynamite.

In his biography of his late brother, Herbert Emmerson Wilson explains what happened next. "Brother Twelve shouted for his followers to halt," he wrote, "but it only helped hasten their departure: most of them began to run. This so infuriated the Guru that he raised his rifle and started firing over their heads. Madame Zee was more dangerous. Dropping to one knee, she took aim and fired at the fleeing cultists. A former lawyer from Montreal received a minor shoulder wound, but the other shots flew wild and no great damage was done."

As the fleeing men and women rowed toward Nanaimo, they heard "numerous booms of explosions drifting from the area behind them, and quickly realized their meaning"--the two remaining on De Courcy Island "were making sure that there would be little or nothing for the police and public to gain when they arrived....As far away as Nanaimo, people could see smoke billowing up in black clouds."

The men and women babbling out what they knew in the police headquarters were proving true what Roger Painter would later put into words. "As I look back...the whole scheme was to drive you into intense fear and confusion," he noted, "so that you was [sic] glad to go and leave your money and goods behind, regardless of what it might cost you."

From the police station the excited men and women proceeded to the law offices of Victor Harrison, where the first complaints were duly filed. Roger Painter estimated that he was out $80,000; Mrs. Connally admitted to $52,000, but the real sum was probably a great deal larger, and the Barleys were out at least $16,000.

There's the stroke. Then came an unexpected counterstroke. Wilson/Brother XII/Amiel de Valdes stormed into his lawyer's office and demanded to know from a flabbergasted Frank Cunliffe how much a defence would cost.

"A great deal," Cunliffe is said to have told the angry man standing before him.

This answer that was really no answer only infuriated Brother XII further. He demanded that Cunliffe name a price. And Cunliffe, who was growing increasingly uneasy, did; it was a large sum. Brother XII made a quick counter-offer and a deal was made on the spot.

From the moment he had opened fire on his departing disciples, Brother XII knew the jig was up. Any seasoned con man could read the signs. Atonement was hours or, at best, days away.

Moving swiftly, the devious pair sold off everything for which they could find a market. William Coats, a resident of nearby Gabriola Island, later related to a Toastmasters Club Christmas party at Yellow Point Lodge, near Cedar, how he purchased 250 tons of material jettisoned by Brother XII as he cleared house on De Courcy.

Working quickly but thoroughly, the two moved not only their own belongings but forty-three crates of gold from their various hiding places onto the *Kheunaten*. Ever prepared to flee, Brother XII had already provisioned the tug for a long sea cruise. Once the vessel was shipshape, the two turned their attention to the last piece of unfinished business-- revenge.

It was swift and sweet. Those who witnessed the results said the process must have bordered on pure madness: savage, wanton, destructive. The watchers also speculated the two were under the influence of drugs of some sort; otherwise, they wondered, how could two humans act in such a manner?

Newspaper reporters wondered the same thing, once the news of what had taken place on the island reached Victoria and Vancouver. Headlines were soon screaming, "A Rampage of Destruction" and Canadians from Tofino to St. John's eagerly bought each edition of their local paper to learn what was happening "out there in the islands."

For many the flaming finale, and the only real tragedy of that furious day of destruction, was the scuttling of the Aquarian Foundation's fleet. The proud and beautiful *Lady Royal* was found demasted at Parrot Cove, the gaping hole below her waterline looking like a wound to the shocked onlookers. Other vessels had been disabled either by being blasted with dynamite or punctured with axes. The scene resembled the aftermath of a major battle.

Cecil Clark, then of the Provincial Police, was the first officer to land on De Courcy Island after the departure of the de Valdes couple. "We went up in Police Boat PML-6 from Ganges [Saltspring Island] with Constable Don Tweedhope at the helm," he reported. "We slipped into the cove one morning. Sergeant Bob Owens, Tweedhope, Constable Bob Marshall and myself rowed ashore to see what was going on."

Once ashore they met Roger Painter, Mary Connally and other colonists who had ventured over the day before. Alfred Barley was doing an inventory of the damage. Clark's account is brief, but agrees with what the newspapers were saying. At the De Courcy farm, they reported, the windows of buildings were smashed, doors were torn from their hinges, water tanks and cisterns had been hacked and punctured, fencing had been ripped up and removed. Even the fruit trees had been uprooted, and fifty walnut trees were missing.

Thus Brother XII was living up to what he had promised his departing colonists: to "weave a ring of death around the witness stand."

Aboard the *Kheunaten*, heartily enjoying the consternation they had left in their wake, Brother XII and his vulgar mistress first visited Roberts Creek, a tiny fishing village on the British Columbia mainland near the pulp-mill town of Powell River. A provincial policeman later visited them at an anchorage near the Yuculta Rapids at Sonora Island, than and now an extremely popular fishing area with American powerboat cruisers.

At Sonora Island, Brother XII's trail ends. It is said that from British Columbia the couple made their way to California, as ever a hotbed of occult activity. From there he went to Australia, and this is confirmed by his brother's understandable if badly engineered attempt to have his brother's history end in that country, under a gravestone bearing the name "Mrs. William Knight." More than likely this is Herbert Wilson's last attempt to cover his brother's trail, perhaps following another successful confidence job in Australia. But then too, according to the younger Wilson, Brother XII buried the ill-gotten gold on De Courcy before he and Madame Zura made their getaway.

In 1939 a more conclusive end came to Brother XII's villainous career. That year a legal advertisement appeared in Vancouver's *Daily Province* announcing the death of one Julian Skottowe in Neuchatel, Switzerland, five years earlier on November 7, 1934. It was assumed by many that Madame Zura had departed with the gold as

Brother XII lay dying.

All these years later, Brother XII's last written message to his followers lives on in Vancouver Island history and legend: "For fools and traitors--NOTHING."

Brother XII's memory won't fade. In the last months of 1988, an article about him appeared in John Robert Colombo's *Mysterious Canada*; a TV program narrated by Pierre Berton appeared on a Canada-wide network; his story was mentioned in *Maclean's*, the Canadian newsmagazine; XII was mentioned several times during that brief period in Vancouver Island newspapers and magazines; and *Canadian West* published an article about him.

Mary Connally lived on Valdes Island until her age and poverty grew too heavy a burden to bear. Most writers have assumed that her once-clear mind had begun to suffer, for her last recorded words were these: "For the old brother, I'd give that much money again, if I had any left to give."

Interlude

What you have just read is a patchwork of the story of Brother XII as it emerges from dozens of interviews, magazine and newspaper articles.

It's one thing to read a well-written magazine article by the likes of Howard O'Hagan or Pierre Berton, writers whose mark on Canadian letters cannot be dismissed; it's quite another to sift through articles and newspaper clippings by the kilo in search of threads that run true.

My wife learned to stop asking me about Brother XII as I emerged from my study for lunch. She knew something was wrong even before I admitted aloud that Brother XII's story was too black to be real; when it wasn't pitch black, it faded away into a wispy grey of dangling surmise. All too often for my comfort, insinuation had replaced fact and gossip was treated as gospel.

What bothered me most was how Brother XII had been consistently dealt with out of context. No one had looked into where he fit in a larger world, the society of those times. In the early days he seems to have been a serious follower of Madame Blavatsky, as was his almost exact contemporary, the Nobel Prize-winning poet William Butler Yeats; like XII, Yeats went on to create his own system. To ignore such parallels, and Yeats was only one of many who come to mind, is to fall into writing propaganda (to give bigotry a less odious name). To write biography and history means following different rules, stricter rules by far. Was Brother XII a con man? One question I had asked a year before, when I was still wanting to believe the popularized legend of Brother XII, was about his past record. Where was it? Everything reinforces XII's claim that he was Edward Arthur Wilson, a retired ship's captain, and rarely do elderly former merchant marine officers turn to criminal careers once ashore.

So much else didn't make sense. His reputation for evil, for instance, faded away like a mirage or rainbow the closer I focussed on it. This reputation, under scrutiny, became as nervous as a whore in church. I couldn't pin anything down.

What triggered my sleuthing for what is commonly taken as truth, what sent me in search of private and public archival material, was rereading various books by and about "the Great Beast," Aleister Crowley, one of this century's great magicians.

Crowley and XII were contemporaries. "I am the Beast," Crowley wrote about himself. "I am the Word of the Aeon. I spend my soul in blazing torrents that roar into Night, streams that with molten tongues hiss as they lick. I am a hell of a Holy Guru." They were magicians, con men, writers and poets, drug and sex addicts, or so I've been told by several Vancouver Islanders who knew something of both men. Yet unlike XII's life, Aleister Crowley's career (whatever one may think of it) is minutely documented. When I started comparing all that Crowley did do and all that XII was supposed to have done, it was like comparing a carefully catalogued gold cartwheel and a copper penny that's been handed around without anyone knowing much about it.

Why haven't our writers, our local history writers, bitten into these full-ripe questions? Brother XII disappeared in 1933, I said to myself. How could I be the first person in almost sixty years to question, really question, the well-worn legend? A year after my initial doubts, I know a major part of the answer: our unthinking belief in the written word is putting us off the track of truth-seeking. Why should anyone doubt what our writers produce, particularly those professional personalities so comfortable with the national media? These men have been paid well for decades to cut through and pronounce on the increasingly entwined complexities of our world. We believe what they say--and if we don't trust them, we ask ourselves, who can we trust?

Our aching need for a folklore of our own is another part of the answer. We want to tell the stories, to embellish and trade the half-familiar tales like a common coastal currency. While watching our children play in a playground just the other night, my friend Greg Evans turned to me and asked what I was writing these days. As a third-generation Nanaimoan, I knew he'd be interested in XII. What I didn't expect was his response.

"I hope you'll tell the truth."

"What's the truth?" I asked.

"My grandmother always maintained that no one started telling Brother XII stories until after the pubs closed."

THE MYSTERY BEYOND
THE LEGEND

"Brother XII" as he appeared in Morton L. Bennett's *The Strange Case of Brother Twelve*. This was the first time a photo of the Brother, XII appeared in print and has proven to be the likeness favoured by two generations of writers. Clearly it is a close-up taken from the group photo

Don Clark Collection.

For the last time the Aquarian faithful pause for the camera. The location is the Nanaimo courthouse, the date April 27, 1933. *Victoria's Daily Colonist* identified these men and women as (left to right): Bruce Crawford, M. Hirst, Mrs. B. Crawford, Miss M. White, Mrs. Mary Connally, R.W. Painter, Mrs. Barley, and A.H. Barley.

Don Clark Collection.

Taken in 1927, this is the only photo to capture the most important of the Aquarian Foundation's thinkers under the famous maple tree. Left to right: Edward A. Lucas, Joseph S. Brenner, Maurice Von Platen, The Brother, XII, P. Jutson Fisher, Will Levington Comfort, Coulson Turnbull. All but Comfort were on the A.F's Board of Directors in 1928.

Don Clark Collection.

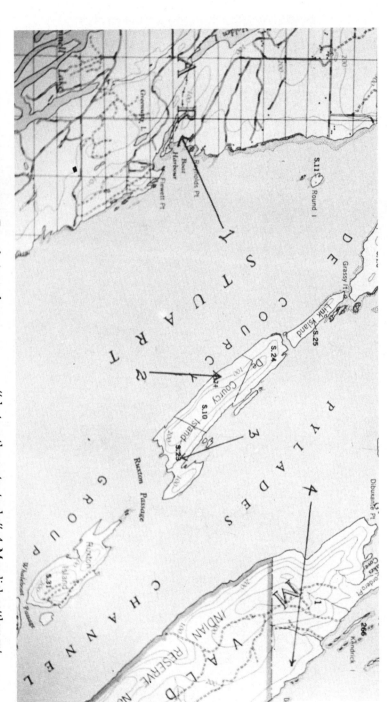

1. The site of the original Aquarian Foundation colony.
2. Mary Connally's house. 3. Sawmill site; here Brother XII "shot up the water tanks". 4. Mandieh settlement.

"The hulk of the once glorious *Lady Royal* lay a smashed and battered thing." This photo first appeared in Bennett's pioneering article in *The Shoulder Strap* in 1941. Was this taken soon after she was blown up, or long afterwards? If Brother XII maintained his "navy" as legend suggests, why is the bottom of the *Lady Royal* covered with barnacles? This is a ship that's long been derelict, not a recently scuttled trawler. *Don Clark Collection.*

After various careers, the *Lady Royal* was indeed a royal lady in 1964.

Cecil Clark Collection.

Brother XII's infamous House of Mystery, home first to Isis and then Madame Zura.

Don Clark Collection.

This is the "shack" Madame Zura forced Georgina Crawford to paint. The history of this photo is unknown, as is the identity of the woman; reportedly the scene was faked for a magazine photographer. In some photographs buildings that look suspiciously like this "shack" are identified as "forts". Scrutiny of this photo reveals the building is neither "fort" nor "shack," but an outhouse. Provenance unknown.

Don Clark Collection.

I

The Beginning of the End

The contradictions, mistakes of fact, flights of fancy and what amounts to outright prevarication in the traditional written record of Brother XII's activities proved to me that I must turn to the court records. On the first page of the first court transcript I made the first of many satisfying breakthroughs.

The hearing between Connally and Brother XII began at 11 a.m. on April 26, 1933, not April 2 as sometimes reported, and as is typed on the court transcript.

It transpires that there was not one trial but two hearings, both in Nanaimo during April 1933. Mary Connally's case against Amiel de Valdes was heard before Justice Morrison on the 26th. The next day, A.H. Barley's case was heard.

Mary Connally's case opened at 11 a.m. and court recessed for lunch at 1 p.m., came to order again at 2:15 and the judgement in favour of Mary Connally was handed down at 4:45 p.m. "Brother Mary" was awarded "judgement for amount claimed, $37,600, less credit for value of lands [De Courcy Island, 400 acres on Valdes Island] $12,000. Judgement for Plaintiff $26,400 [sic], Judgement for Plaintiff for $10,000 damages."

The official transcript or verbatim does little to support the version of this hearing published under the headline, "Aquarian Foundation Suit Lost by 'Brother Twelve' in the Supreme Court" in the *Nanaimo Daily Free Press*. A slightly different version of this article appeared in Victoria's *Colonist* on April 27, 1933.

"The most amazing story ever told in a Canadian court," the anonymous reporter gushes, "was unfolded to Chief Justice Morrison here yesterday, as witness after witness related details of life under Brother XII, otherwise Edward Arthur Wilson, but now known as Amiel de Valdes, who claimed to be the personal Chela of a divinity ruling fortified islands and armed guards. Strange rites, peculiar happenings and conditions described as equaling the worst features of penal colonies or slave compounds of olden times were described in the testimony of a dozen witnesses, and in documents filed during the hearing of the claim of Mrs. Mary W. T. Connally, former society leader of Ashville, North Carolina, against de Valdes and his co-workers and Chief Assistant Zura de Valdes."

I started work on the end of the paragraph above. From the first summons (dated Sept. 24, 1932), the case had been between Mary W.T. Connally and Amiel de Valdes and Zura de Valdes. Nowhere are any "co-workers" mentioned. The "documents filed during the hearing" that describe and (one assumes) support the testimony of the "dozen witnesses" are as follows: five books written by The Brother, XII; twelve issues of *The Chalice;* one folder of letters; a letter dated 16.7.32 to Wilson/de Valdes; a letter from "The Brother to Lady Mary" dated 30.1.31; a note from Mary Connally in reply; "Letter Lady Mary to Z 8.9.31"; two cheques for $1504.07 and $500; and, finally, abstracts of land title.

As I hunched over that list with a high-power lamp and a magnifying glass to decipher the court registrar's handwriting, I realized that nothing in this inventory could confirm the "strange rites...penal colonies or slave compounds" mentioned by the newspaper. Next I noted that there were not the often-reported "dozen" witnesses, but only ten: Mary Connally, Annie Barley, William Lowell, Bruce Crawford, Leona Painter, Ada Gertrude Phillips, Mary Lowell, Georgina Crawford, Fred Hernishner and Alfred H. Barley.

The seldom-used proper name for our central figure is this: The Brother, XII. That his stronghold was fortified, as the article in the *Nanaimo Daily Free Press* claimed, and that there were armed guards, there is no doubt. The testimony is very clear on these points.

After the material already quoted, there follows a brief description of the judgement for the plaintiff. Approximately half of the remaining text (and this anonymous article in April '33 might fill about four full columns in any contemporary large-city daily) is a rehash of the articles covering the 1928 trial, when Robert England disappeared, and various articles that had appeared in the interim.

The plaintiff's lawyer, Victor Harrison, "brought out a most amazing sidelight through skillful questioning of witnesses," crowed the *Free Press* reporter. "It had to do with a young man named Carlin Ruddle and his wife, a girl in her early twenties." The reporter then proceeded to provide his readers with the sordid details that would appear repeatedly in rehashed versions of this story for the next sixty-one years. What the reporter doesn't bother to explain is that he got most of his story outside the courtroom. Chief Justice Morrison refused to listen to hearsay evidence, so the

Ruddle story was never told in court, and the witnesses' veracity was never challenged.

It is discouraging to turn back to the claims made by the tall-tale account of this trial. The only mention of gold amounts to little more than $500 in gold coin sent to Brother XII by one couple. There is no mention of "black magic," "sorcery", "strange invocations recovered from the ruins of Egypt." The "complete mastery of one mind over eight thousand" is never mentioned.

The judgement awarded Mary Connally--some land, $10,000 damages and $26,400--does not suggest that Lady Mary "had been bled for countless thousands of dollars."

Next I concentrated on some of the most baffling points exposed at Mary Connally's hearing. Under cross-examination, Mary Connally admitted that the exodus from Valdes Island took place on March 17, 1931, but "there were no steps taken" by her "until August 1932." Is this period of seventeen months the hiatus, the period of indecision, Victor Harrison had meant when he admitted to writer Bruce McKelvie that he doubted whether he could get his clients to press charges?

Fear of Brother XII's magic may have been in Mary Connally's mind when she told the defence attorney, "I was still under their mental domination." Maybe--but as I worked through the documents and a pile of letters no one else had consulted, I began to believe that the investigation of this mental domination question was going to be a good deal more enticing than the emerging picture of The Brother, XII.

Back in court the defence lawyer was cross-examining Mary Connally about Roger Painter, who the group at Cedar-by-the-Sea had begun calling Brother IX. Judge Morrison interrupted defence attorney Frank Cunliffe: "As I understand it, there is no complaint whatever by this lady about anything except the fact that these defendants used all this whatever-it-may-be-called as a medium to defraud them, and now they have left and disappeared after imposing upon them and stealing their money and destroying their property, they are still there and still thankful and still believe; and it is not for me or for you to make any comment about their belief, and there is no point as to what their belief is; whatever it is, the allegation is that these two people went to work and took advantage of these people's beliefs and defrauded them, shamefully and cruelly, and then abandoned them. It doesn't matter what her belief is. I wouldn't understand it if you went into it; and why take up the time?"

Cunliffe's cross-questioning did reveal that Lady Mary's accounting could not stand up to an audit. In making her claim she had forgotten, or wished to ignore, that one $1500 sum she said had been given to The Brother, XII, had actually been paid, by her, for Cunliffe's legal services when defending The Brother, XII against Robert England's charges in 1928. It was an awkward turn of events.

Judge Morrison announced he did not wish to hear this matter discussed. But Cunliffe, realizing it "cast some reflection on his honour as a practitioner," to use plaintiff's counsel Victor Harrison's words, met with Harrison during the lunch recess. Then and there he proved to Harrison's satisfaction that Mary Connally had paid him, and that he had not high-handedly taken the money from a larger sum given to him for another purpose. Much to Judge Morrison's disgust, Harrison brought up the discussion immediately after court resumed at 2:15 p.m.; Harrison nonetheless dropped the $1500 from Mary Connally's claim.

Another $1500 Mary Connally was claiming, this time for money she'd given to Brother XII to pay for "engines" in a tug he was building, came under scrutiny. She could not remember the exact date ("in the winter of 1928-29") nor exactly how she'd given Brother XII the money. Although she thought it might have been by cheque, she could not produce this piece of paper.

Highlights titillating enough to make the courtroom audience sit up and gasp, as they supposedly did, do not shine brightly at all in the court record. Not even in the papers filed by Mary Connally is there information that can't be found elsewhere.

At the time she started the proceedings, the report I found revealed this: "The defendant, Amiel de Valdes, resides on the De Courcy Islands, in the said Country, and is a retired mariner, and at the times hereinafter mentioned sometimes went by his original name of Edward Arthur Wilson, and at other times went under the designation of "The Brother XII," and since the 23rd. day of March [sic], A.D., 1931, by deed poll, changed his name to Amiel de Valdes, by which latter name the said defendant is now known.

"The defendant, Zura de Valdes, resides on the De Courcy islands, in the said Country, and at times hereinafter mentioned was known as Mabel Rowbotham, Mabel Skottowe, and Zura de Valdes, which last mentioned name was assumed by deed poll dated the 23rd. day of September, 1931, and is a married woman."

As Judge Morrison suggested in his long comment interrupting Cunliffe's cross-examination of Mary Connally, fraud--and nothing else--was the crime being dealt with in this particular hearing. Mary Connally admitted that she had sent the initial $2,000 to The Brother, XII as a direct result of reading his book, *Foundation Letters and Teachings*. She was also deeply influenced by his first book, *Three Truths*, and by the material subsequently published in *The Chalice*. For reasons best known to herself, she chose to quote one paragraph from the preface of *Three Truths* in her Statement of Claim, a writ issued by the plaintiff on September 24, 1932: "Being written to many individuals and in the midst of swiftly-moving events, they present a picture of the gradual unfoldment of this Work of The White Lodge, or rather of those stages of the Work which have so far been made public."

This is the sort of material Judge Morrison did not want examined and cross-examined in his court. He wanted everyone to stick to the issue of fraud. Pierre Berton, in his discussion of The Brother, XII's religious beliefs, referred to them as being "evil" and "kooky"-- an odd pairing of words.

The same sort of esoterica is likely still irking contemporary Judge Morrisons. A brief excerpt from Elizabeth Clare Prophet's *The Chela and the Path*, from Summit University Press, is a 1976 example. "*The Chela and the Path* contains the teachings of the Ascended Master El Morya which he dictated to me at my retreat in Santa Barbara," she writes. "In it he presents a step-by-step analysis of the Greater Self and the lesser self, drawing the threads of reality and truth handed down from the Ancient of Days. . . . the law of life taught by the ascended masters . . . in the retreats of the Great White Brotherhood."

A much earlier example comes from Madame Blavatsky, founder of theosophy and prolific author whose works still command attention. "There are strange traditions," she writes, "current in various parts of the East --on Mount Athos and in the Desert of Nitria, for instance--among certain monks , and with learned Rabbis in Palestine, who pass their lives in commenting upon the Talmud. They say that not all the rolls and manuscripts reported in history to have been burned by Caesar, by the Christian mob, in 389 . . . perished as it is commonly believed." Though she died before 1900, more than forty of her books remain in print.

In a thoughtful article published some years ago, novelist Kurt Vonnegut, Jr. wrote: "Madame Blavatsky has plenty of followers still. Her most important contribution to American intellectual history is this, it seems to me: she encouraged a lot of Yankees to suspect that spooky aspects of foreign religions might not be the claptrap scientists said they were."

Madame Blavatsky, once described as "a mannish, aggressively celibate Russian noblewoman," stands at the beginning of the theosophical movement as we know it today; Elizabeth Clare Prophet is touring among us now. Between these two stands Edward Arthur Wilson, writing in the 1920s.

Wilson's message was important to some. The Alfred Barleys never repudiated The Brother, XII's early teachings, nor did any of the other Aquarian Foundation stalwarts, so far as we know. And Mary Connally never ceased doubting The Brother, XII's writings. She made it very clear why she was taking him to court in 1933. He lied to her, she said, though it was called "falsely representing to the plaintiff" by her lawyer, Victor Harrison.

I knew I had to cut through a lot of nonsense written before his time and since. What appealed to so many of the men and women who joined the Aquarian Foundation was the very fact of joining a theosophical brotherhood where the young would be taught love and respect--older values. To most this meant teaching the children pre-1914 standards, and that is why the Foundation was doomed from the start. It could not attract the young, only the older generation--men like Alfred Barley and women like Mary Connally, both in their 60s--who wanted to maintain the status quo of their formative years.

The trial was concerned with fraud in that The Brother, XII had not kept his word, had not followed his own teachings. Mary Connally and the Barleys wanted their money back so they could continue living and working along the principles he himself had outlined. This trial had nothing to do with good versus evil, "slave compounds," stolen or buried gold, sex, magic or murder.

If, like me, you have spent years living with the ever-flowing tale of Brother XII or, worse, of "Brother Twelve," understanding the implications of this takes time. But once it is understood, what follows makes a good deal of sense.

II

The Man Who Never Was

From the beginning, narrow-focus publishers and wide-eyed innocence have plagued the subject of The Brother, XII, and his writings and the various attempts at his biography.

Untangling facts from fabrications has had its less than noble moments. One publisher who read an early draft of my manuscript drew large question marks next to almost every name in the first fifty pages, whereupon he apparently gave up and shipped it back. Another publisher mumbled over and over during our discussion of this book: "But Pierre Berton didn't say that."

That tepid resistance was only one element in my curious odyssey as I worked to piece together the real story of The Brother, XII. Another was the attitude many people adopted as I questioned them about their Brother XII stories. Most discounted any evidence I showed them as unimportant, once again reminding me that many well-educated people still believe that emotional responses carry the same weight as documented facts.

What has intrigued me most is our collective lack of curiosity. Brother XII was painted black as soot in the 1930s and he has remained black. No one ever apparently cared enough about the truth to ask any important questions or to look again through the actual documents.

California writer and professor James A. Santucci commented during our phone conversation, "Wilson's a true magus--we know nothing about him." Think of another magus, the mysterious character Conchis at the core of *The Magus*, that immensely popular novel by John Fowles. For some, the major character in the book is a magician or sorcerer, or--whatever each person believes Conchis to be, one moment to the next.

The difference between these two magi is that Brother XII remains a mystery mainly because our historians haven't done their research; Fowles' magus never stepped from the literary twilight.

It was a year ago that Santucci and I discussed the problems of writing about Wilson. I now know something of the man's movements, though, to my regret, breathing life into random facts and figures, into corrections and niceties, is a far tougher job than braiding the same sort of information into an imaginative novel. The satisfaction must lie in the questioning.

By the remarkably simple expedient of writing to the Swiss authorities, for instance, I learned that The Brother, XII was Edward Arthur Wilson, born in Birmingham, England, on July 25, 1878. Although the man who died may not be The Brother, XII/Brother XII (a point we will return to later), this information about the man who was alive was almost certainly taken verbatim from a passport. The Swiss authorities would not be so sure of their information were their source not official. His parents were Thomas Wilson and Sarah Ellen (nee Pearsal) Wilson. At the time of his death in Neuchatel, Switzerland, November 7, 1934, Wilson was listed as celibataire -- a bachelor.

His mother's name puts to the sword the idea that his mother was of royal Kasmiri birth. Just as Alfred Barley suggested in a letter to Bruce McKelvie long ago, in all likelihood Thomas Wilson was in one way or another affiliated with the Irvingites. This group is named after Edward Irving (1792 - 1818), a Scottish minister and one of the great orators of his time; he was as well a founder of the Catholic Apostolic Church. Except for its orders of apostles, prophets, evangelists, pastors and angels, and its much admired ritualistic service and elaborate liturgy, the Irvingites do not differ in dogma from the Catholic Church.

The Brother, XII made no secret of his knowledge of this group. In "Things We Ought to Know," one of his first-published articles in England, I found him discussing the experiences of the Irvingites. His father Thomas Wilson's position within this group is not known. There were fifty thousand members at the turn of the century, and thus far Thomas's name has not been traced. If he were an Irvingite minister, this might explain the younger Wilson's later dislike of the Catholic Church. Curiously--like father like son--the Aquarians and the Irvingites shared a belief (even though it differed in specifics) in a second coming. The first group thought it would occur in 1847, the latter in 1975.

No evidence to the contrary has emerged to disprove the six decades' old contention that son Edward ran away to sea, or went to sea early in his life. There is no record of this, but this may be due more to not knowing where to look than to the documents not existing.

Compounding this is the growing official attitude in the United

States, Canada and England that if you are not dealing firmly within academic channels, you're not worth the bother. There have been a number of peculiar glitches. One Californian research centre, in response to questions about back copies of shipping directories, sent in return an application form to join a geneological society. In British Columbia, one government department charges Canadian individuals for research work but does the work free for American academics. A cheque for twelve pounds sterling was sent back to me from Britain because, the letter said, "we can only accept cheques made out in sterling." Despite those and other burrs, there has been factual progress.

It is a well-documented fact that Wilson sailed the *Lady Royal*, described by the newspapers of the time as "a small sailing vessel of twenty-five tons," from England to Cedar-by-the-Sea almost single-handedly. He had with him a two-man crew and his ladylove, Zura de Valdes. It seems from this feat that he was indeed a mariner, just as he claimed.

Sometime around 1900-1910, Wilson supposedly reached Victoria and lived there for 'years,' employed at the Dominion Express then located at 1104 Government Street. Bruce McKelvie wrote that some time immediately prior to the 1928 trial in Nanaimo, Brother XII had been confronted by someone who had known him as a Victoria-based clerk. McKelvie never revealed the name of the man who recognized Wilson.

However much one wants to believe McKelvie, there is no paper documentation to back up the story of this encounter between Wilson and someone who had known him in Victoria. What isn't generally known is that McKelvie makes it clear in a letter that his witness had also known Wilson in Calgary. This is an important detail.

Howard O'Hagan wrote that Herbert Wilkinson had known Wilson in Victoria when he was a clerk. Wilkinson is no longer listed in Victoria phone books. No matter: the late O'Hagan's papers tell us that Wilkinson's sole comments were brief--that in 1912 Wilson was about twenty-five years old, about 145 pounds, slim and a "smooth-talker." As there is no street number but only a phone number next to this jotting, I suspect that the "interview" was a phone conversation.

Of course, the impressions related by Wilkinson may be absolutely true, but was the man Wilkinson worked with at the Dominion Express office really Edward Arthur Wilson or was he Julian Skottowe, a man who was remarkably similar in appearance? It's an identification that might have been further confused by Wilson's living with Skottowe's wife; this is not the only time the Wilson and Skottowe masks will have overlapped, deliberately or accidentally.

If one has doubts about McKelvie's source and about O'Hagan's, the same nagging uncertainties apply to Gwen Cash's source, Wilson's sailing friend. None of these informants provides us with material that can be checked against other sources. Since this sort of thing wouldn't be allowed in a court of law, why should it be treated as anything other than hearsay in our quest for The Brother, XII?

Furthermore, I found it strange that only two old men remembered Wilson in the 1950s and 1960s, while back in the 1920s, less than ten or fifteen years after he'd supposedly left Victoria, only one unnamed person recognized him.

Wilson claimed in his *Foundation Letters and Teachings*, published in 1927, that sometime in 1912 he had "passed through a Ceremony of Dedication; then it was that I understood that I had a work to do, but did not know anything of its nature or when it was to be. This was followed by twelve chaotic years of testing and wandering in all parts of the world. Outwardly I was unsuccessful in everything I did, but the inner work or preparation must have been going quietly on."

Edward Arthur Wilson next appears in California--at Ocean Beach, to be exact--on May 16, 1915, according to the records of the American Theosophical Society. By June 9, 1916, his theosophical mail was being sent c/o S.R. Maxwell and Company, Papeete, Tahiti. A year later he was back on the U.S. West Coast and living in San Diego. These authenticated addresses make it almost impossible for Wilson to have served in the Royal Navy or in the U.S. Merchant Marine on the Atlantic Ocean during World War I, as is frequently claimed. Records show he joined the society on January 6, 1913, and remained a member until June 30, 1918.

Coulson Turnbull, writing in July 1928 from Cedar, claimed that, "Some nine years have passed since I first met the writer of these history-making articles [*The End of the Days*, published in 1928]. Our seeming casual acquaintance deepened into a warm, quiet friendship, although neither obtruded himself on the other more than occasion required. My new friend, I discovered was an 'Old Friend,' a worker in a Group whose lineage reaches far back into distant ages."

Turnbull and Wilson had discovered they were both theosophists--the group "whose lineage reaches far back . . . ." The friendship would seem to date back to 1919, and probably began in

California. Wilson refers several times in his published writings to California having been his home for years.

Will Levington Comfort can be tracked at least to Cedar, but Coulson Turnbull and the other authors and publishers who worked with The Brother, XII, *The Chalice Press,* and *The Chalice* between the summer of 1927 and September 1928, have proven to be untraceable through various directories, through back editions of *Who's Who,* *Who Was Who,* the *Dictionary of National Biography,* and the many existing biographical dictionaries featuring writers. This perhaps means nothing more than that as writers and publishers, they were small potatoes. Will Levington Comfort was quite a different story.

Various authors have claimed that in 1924 Wilson was at Nanaimo, that he was broke and unable to pay his room-and-board bill. He reassured his landlady that she shouldn't worry, that he would return soon as the head of a new religion and she'd have her money then.

Everyone who's touched this story has mauled it in one way or another. What strikes me as strange is that this landlady, named by some as Peggy Reynolds, was never interviewed and was never mentioned in the 1920s and 1930s; her role did not emerge until the 1950s. And as a woman by that name did live in Nanaimo in 1928, I wonder why she never spoke up, and why no one bothered to interview her.

Early in the first section of this book I quoted Brother XII's own account starting: "In 1924 while staying at a small place in the South of France and quite alone...." There is no reason to disbelieve Wilson's own account, since in sixty-one years none of it has been proven a lie.

We do know that early in May 1926 he set out from Genoa for England. It was at this time that his first known articles began appearing in *The Occult Review,* thought by some to be "the best general occult periodical in the English language." These publications mark the beginning of what would become the Aquarian Foundation. By September 15, 1926, his address was "care of R.M. Sedgwich, 'Melrose,' Keymer, Hassocks, Sussex, England."

Two months later he took another step forward and began signing himself: "Your Brother in Service, XII. (The Master's personal Chela)." All correspondence to XII was to be sent to "E.A. Wilson, 18 Erskine Road, London, E. 17, England."

As though to reassure his listeners, XII concludes his first known message to his Canadian readers with this statement:
"THE MESSAGE IS EVERYTHING, THE PERSONALITY OF THE MESSENGER IS NOTHING. ON THE ACCEPTANCE OF THE

MESSAGE ITSELF, ALL MUST STAND OR FALL."

And signs off, "Peace be to all Beings."

Alfred and Annie Barley met Wilson-XII and his wife Alma in the Wilsons' Southampton rooms on January 5, 1927. Like many theosophists and religious leaders, XII was an inspired organizer. Between January 5 and sometime in March, when the Wilsons and Barleys sailed for Montreal, XII held numerous meetings. He convinced the Barleys to pack up their belongings and sell their property, and started contacting his West Coast connections.

While in Ottawa he delivered a talk to theosophists, the text of which still survives. The four reached Nanaimo in April 1927, and Wilson began creating his new infrastructure and contacting various connections. The Societies Act of British Columbia/the Aquarian Foundation/Declaration was filed in the County of Nanaimo on the 30th of April, 1927.

Although we know that Wilson-XII made a quick train trip to California shortly after he and the Barleys reached Northfield on Vancouver Island, I feel that he was either one tremendous salesman or, more likely, that he had known many of these people (and Turnbull admits to his long friendship with Wilson) for many years. If this is true, it follows that these were the people to whom he implies he was writing before he left Genoa for England.

And where does this leave Herbert Emmerson Wilson's "biography" of his brother? Out in the cold. As many have long known, and as John Robert Colombo wrote in his *Mysterious Canada* about that so-called biography, *Canada's False Prophet*, "The biography was 'ghost' written by the pulp writer Thomas P. Kelley."

This in itself proves nothing. For information of a different kind we must turn to *Saturday Night* magazine, the issue dated March 15, 1952. Under the heading "Story of A Canadian Safecracker" there runs an article informing us that the preacher-brother of Edward Arthur Wilson was Canada's "ex-King of the Safecrackers." He was a thief who spent "twelve years in San Quentin Prison," the article continues, and claimed to have amassed "a fortune of $15,000,000 as a bank robber in the United States, from which he was deported in 1935 after serving his time."

We are turned around yet again.

III

Probability's Thin Edge

Edward Arthur Wilson/XII/Brother XII/The Brother, XII knew of Cedar-by-the-Sea and Vancouver Island, and I wanted to find out how.

If we believe the legendary account, it happened something like this. Early in 1926 in Southampton, Wilson announced that the message was coming in, the time was nigh. The Masters, he told the assemblage gathered at his feet, were now prepared to reveal the chosen sanctuary. With ceremony befitting the occasion, the white-robed Chela of the Master proceeded with the samadhi ritual that, he claimed, transported his spirit through the outer world and into the halls of the Great White Lodge.

This sounds good. Witnesses said that the session lasted an hour or more, during which time a perspiration-soaked XII twisted, convulsed and babbled incoherently. He emerged holding a map drawn for him by the Brothers of the Great White Circle.

"On it," Annie Barley was to claim later, "were plainly marked the islands, inlets and narrow seaways off the coast of British Columbia. Brother XII told us this was to be our place of refuge."

While the terminology is right, and while all of this can be found in the writings of Madame Blavatsky, the performance is all wrong. Wilson's earlier psychic experiences sound normal enough, within this framework, but the term "samadhi" means profound meditation. It's the final Yoga state in which the meditator becomes one with his meditation. This is superconsciousness. What Annie Barley and others have described as happening in Wilson's Southampton rooms that day was hardly samadhi. At best, it was a shamanic performance, and at worst it was something more at home in a carnival.

Was this what actually occurred? Would Wilson, a knowledgeable theosophist himself, stand up before half a dozen or more other theosophists and put on such a show? Or was Annie Barley merely remembering what gossips and journalists said took place? She might not have been there at all. Stranger things happen.

An acquaintance of mine who has been involved in settling disputes concerning WWI military pensions revealed recently that a surprising number of the claimants believe they were overseas during the Great War, even though the records say these men never left Canada. Now, these claimants are not necessarily trying to cheat the system and nor are they liars; they are swept up in one of the oldest mental processes known to man. At first, they listened to veterans tell their stories. Then they told these stories themselves. And then, after many years, they themselves became the heroes of those same stories. Poets call this metamorphosis, acknowledging by naming the process what a time-honoured change of mind it is.

If Annie Barley's memory cannot be trusted, are we to believe that the map produced by Wilson was one of the Strait of Georgia, indeed an Admiralty chart as some have said? There is room for doubt. In one little-known version, Wilson's wife Alma points not to Nanaimo and Cedar-by-the-Sea on Vancouver Island but to Hope, another British Columbia community entirely, on the mainland. Edward Alexander Lucas, a Vancouver lawyer and one of the first governors of the Aquarian Foundation, later claimed that their second choice for settling down was a desolate and logged-off area north of Nanaimo.

Even if Wilson did choose Vancouver Island's east coast in advance, this cannot be read as even the slightest suggestion that the stories of his having clerked in Victoria are true. Wilson claimed to be a retired mariner. He could have worked on ships that travelled the Inside Passage of the British Columbia and Alaska. He may have worked on transpacific vessels that called at Victoria and Vancouver or, like tens of thousands of others during the teens and early '20s, Wilson may have visited Vancouver Island as a tourist.

Equally feasible is that somewhere in California, Wilson encountered the novelist Stewart Edward White, a writer whose interest in theosophy and spiritualism had deepened since his return from overseas duty with the 144th Field Artillery during WWI. White began publishing his findings in 1925; *The Unobstructed Universe*, which White published in 1940, is still in print and is touted as "an unparalleled report of life after death." His best-known psychic books were written too late to have influenced Wilson, but this may not be important.

The two men may well have known each other. Both were interested in spiritualism, both were of about the same age living in the same general area of Southern California. Each had a life-long love affair with boats and sailing. Even if they did not meet, it is quite possible that Wilson read two of White's many novels, *Skookum Chuck* and *Secret Harbor*. Published in 1925 and 1926, the books are largely set along the coast of the Inside Passage between Victoria and the northern end of Vancouver Island--an area White knew intimately after having cruised that coast for years.

To continue my "what if" connection: one leading character in *Skookum Chuck* is X. Anaxagoras, the "Healer of Souls," and the hero is a man who has "been seeking a cure" for the weariness of his soul. The theme is one that would attract The Brother, XII's attention, immediately, it being the thread running so true through everything we know of Wilson/The Brother, XII.

One solid fact was emerging as I continued wrestling with the research. Edward Arthur Wilson's world, as far as the facts have so far outlined it, is one trailing a tangle of threads, many of which we can never hope to unravel. A number of illustrative passages in John H. Watson's Holmesian novel *The Case of the Philosopher's Ring* show how interwoven the world of theosophy, poetry, philosophy and the occult could be in Wilson's time. It was possible, and historically probable, for Aleister Crowley, W.B. Yeats, John Maynard Keynes, Virginia Woolf, the philosophers Russell, Whitehead, Wittgenstein and Moore, Annie Besant, and Sherlock Holmes all to have been in the same town at the same time. And why not? Many were friends, some were working associates, several were lovers.

The biographical confusion deepens on North America's Pacific coast when we try to decipher possible connections among the various theosophical colonies in California, and with Aimee Semple McPherson, her Four Square Gospel Church and the other religious groups. Into the ideological stew add the movie colony in Los Angeles, the literary groups in San Francisco, the art colonies at places like Carmel.

These people who lived by wit and imagination would have been Wilson's immediate contemporaries. Some of these men and women had religious answers to give the public, or they were seeking such answers. As one writer expressed it: "The Twenties had an obvious need for heroes. The abounding materialism, the new wealth, the luxury, the indulgent living, and the rapidly chang-ing moral standards may have made Americans feel uneasy and a bit guilty as they looked back over their shoulders to their more sober past."

On reading this passage, I turned to Brother XII's first known publication. Writing as E.A. Chaylor (could Chaylor be "chela," slightly disguised?) in *The Shadow* in 1926, he said: "'Whom the

Gods would destroy they first make mad.' Surely this wise old adage has a significant and sinister bearing on the condition of the world today. To every thoughtful man, our world appears to be drifting towards madness. The old restraints are being removed or ignored, while license and extravagances are apparent on every hand."

From this he quickly moved to specifics: "Startling clothes, freak fashions, jazz music, cubist and futurist pictures, meaningless 'poetry'; these are but a few of the more obvious and least harmful symptoms. In the ceaseless rush for amusement, for excitement; in the mania for speed and every form of excess, we find an indication of the real nature of the psychic malady which has infected every class and invaded every activity to-day. Through one and all runs the high, harsh, strident note of insanity."

Writing in 1931 and from a different perspective, writer Frederick Lewis Allen claimed: "All nations, in all eras of history, are swept from time to time by waves of contagious excitement over fads or fashions or dramatic public issues. But the size and frequency of these waves is highly variable, as is the nature of events which set them in motion. One of the striking characteristics of the era of Coolidge Prosperity was the unparalleled rapidity and unanimity with which millions of men and women turned their attention, their talk, and their emotional interest upon a series of tremendous trifles--a heavyweight boxing match, a murder trial, a new automobile model, a transatlantic flight."

Was Wilson over-reacting when he saw in this situation the need for a Second Coming? Was White under-reacting when he called the events that led to an immense economic depression and a second world war the "Ballyhoo Years"? Maybe it doesn't matter how we judge either of them. We know that Wilson, White, Hitler, Mussolini, Franklin Delano Roosevelt and thousands of others reacted to the absurdities of the 1920s in a variety of ways--some good, some not so good, some criminal.

In his writing of this period, Wilson/XII makes the claim that, "All events of importance are governed by unchanging Cyclic Law. In accordance with that Law we have entered a period in which the existing order must be dissolved." One worldwide best-seller at the time Wilson wrote those lines was *Der Untergang des Abendlandes--* Oswald Spengler's *The Decline of the West.*

Published in 1924, Spengler's book maintains that history is cyclic, that each of the major races or civilizations go through similar cycles to that of mankind's: birth, youth, middle age, and so on.

Laughed at by some, praised by others (a situation that still continues deep within academic circles), Spengler went on to claim that European civilization was moving into its last years, and that what would come next would be the civilization of the Eastern peoples--the so-called yellow hordes.

William Butler Yeats, by this time a world-famous poet and dramatist, Nobel Prize winner and long-time theosophist, created his own cyclic theory of history in *A Vision* and wrote about it in many poems.

This exploration of the sensibilities of that era may or may not be particularly entertaining, but it serves a point: thus far, I have not uncovered any solid evidence matching the person "Edward Arthur Wilson" to the religious leader "Brother XII". Much of what I have found, however, suggests Wilson was in fact The Brother, XII, a serious theosophist and thinker. He defined himself so clearly and worked so hard at getting his message across that I'm reminded of what Kurt Vonnegut, Jr. said about Madame Blavatsky: "The only greed I can detect in the woman is a greed to be believed."

Here's The Brother, XII proclaiming his message, and it's one with which many might agree: "In the year 1875 H.P. Blavatsky headed a great movement for the regeneration of spiritual life and principles. The ideal of Universal Brotherhood was held up before all nations. Men were shown their common origin, and the unity of their true interests. They were implored to cease from campaigns of mutual hatred and injury, and to make peace. The Message was rejected, and the Messenger practically hounded to her death. The old games of international murder, and lying, and land-grabbing went on unchecked. Commercial immorality increased to an extent unknown before. Class hatreds became more embittered, and Science multiplied the engines of death and destruction."

If we grant Edward Arthur Wilson his theosophical premises, some of it may appear "kooky" but nothing about it is "evil," though he may justifiably be thought of as a crank on gold, Catholics and Jews. My own grandfather's first cousin was equally cranky, but on the subject of silver was something of a religious nut and fought against the teaching of evolution in the U.S. school system. Still, the Democrats ran him for president three times. He didn't impress my grandfather much, however, and most of our family continued to think of William Jennings Bryan as a slow-water Baptist and something of an embarrassment.

Why didn't Vancouver Islanders react against The Brother, XII and not against men such as Matti Kurikka, a socialist free-love advocate and leader of the Sointula colony a few dozen miles upcoast from Cedar-by-the-Sea? One simple answer may be that Kurikka was a foreigner, writing in a foreign language, so his message missed the locals.

Why didn't someone react to the spiritualism that L. Adams Beck was pouring into her fantastically popular novels written from Victoria? Well, Beck was British, a woman with her own record of success; her grandfather, Fairfax Moresby, had been Admiral of the Fleet, and an uncle, Commander Prevost, was responsible for charting much of B.C.'s coast; her father was Admiral John Moresby.

As in many communities, pedigree mollifies public opinion of outright eccentricity. No editor would have dared publish disparaging material about her, nor would any journalist of the day have been so naive as to write such an article. Though L. Adams Beck wrote more than thirty novels and studies in Victoria, lived there for ten years, and was world-famous, not one Victoria paper wrote about her.

One Vancouver Island novelist used The Brother, XII as the archetype for an Irish religious fanatic who brings a village of dupes along to serve him. It's good fun--but being an Islander, the author knew he could get away with his version locally only if he portrayed the man as a fanatic, the dupes as stereotypically Irish and the straight men as English. The novel is a good example of how freewheeling reality can be tucked tidily into fictional proportions.

British though Wilson was, Brother XII was rumoured to be part East Indian, not then one of British Columbia's popular minorities. He was a nobody. Besides, he was secretive, intelligent and proved time and time again to have more chutzpah than the locals. This combination constituted a proclamation of open season on The Brother, XII's skin-- once rumour had made Wilson "Brother XII" (the storytellers' invented character) and not The Brother, XII, the man in fact.

IV

An Aquarian Eden

Nothing demonstrably factual has been written about the first year and a half of the Aquarian Foundation's time at Cedar-by-the-Sea. The heart of what's been published about this early period has been outlined in earlier chapters of this book. We do know that from everything that was later said by the Barleys and other long-time colonists, it was a peaceful time.

As documentation, we have only The Brother, XII's lengthy definition of his organization, the Societies Act as declared by the Foundation early in 1927, and a brief but prolix account of his discovery of the Foundation by Will Levington Comfort. Together, they provide for the first time an official portrait of this period at Cedar-by-the-Sea.

Will Levington Comfort is the only Aquarian whose biography turns up in standard reference books. Born in Michigan in 1878, he spent most of his life after 1918 in Southern California and died there in 1932. Comfort was a war correspondent, a novelist, occultist and journalist. "Though not a member of any particular sect," one writer explained, "he was strongly influenced by occultism, and reviewers often complained that the objectivity of his fiction was blurred by his tendency to mysticism and his insistence upon his social doctrines."

What Comfort's social doctrines might have been is not discussed, though he seems to have been something of a pacifist, outwardly a novel choice for someone who spent a great deal of his life reporting on wars. Writer and editor H.L. Mencken, never one to mince words, claimed that Comfort "has done, indeed, some capital melodramas. What Comfort preaches is a sort of mellowed mariolatry, a humourless exaltation of women." It may have been Comfort's social and occult concerns that drew him to The Brother, XII's teachings, while judging from Mencken's comments, the Isis-Osiris affair drove him away.

It was a clean break, for Comfort's name was never again to be associated with the Foundation after 1928. It had been quite a different matter in 1926. "Lying before the fire," Comfort later wrote, "I read the *'Message of the Masters'* in 1926--Thursday, the 16th of December, before daylight. I did not work on a story that day. Before eight o'clock, I had been through the pamphlet two or three times. One of my associates then came and the Message was read again slowly aloud."

Serious as Comfort is here, he is not without a lighter touch. "Some of its outer garmenture I hadn't liked," he continues. "'Personal Chela' for instance, and I had long noticed that the sentence 'He that hath ears let him hear' isn't particular who uses it." But Comfort admits he "drew in past that, personal gusts of like and dislike not blowing out the flame."

The Brother, XII, as the date on this statement makes clear, was in contact with a California audience even before meeting the Barleys. (The first 'students' to join The Brother, XII, Alfred and Annie Barley met him in Southampton on January 5, 1927.) Coulson Turnbull was undoubtedly his California promoter. Correspondence dated July 19, 1927 between a Mrs. Esther Crawford in Taos, New Mexico, and The Brother, XII (although the letter was signed by Edward Alexander Lucas) establishes Turnbull as the Aquarian Foundation's "Divisional Secretary" in the U.S. Southwest.

Comfort heard of the Foundation through Turnbull, but he was basing his thoughts on his discovery of *'The Message of the Masters'*, an amazingly scarce pamphlet "addressed to all earnest people." It announced "the fact that the Masters of Wisdom are about to do a further Work in the world, that Their plans are already complete, and that the work has now commenced upon the physical plane."

These reflections are valuable as a writer's reaction, and as a student's. Beyond this is its historic importance as the only detailed account of how The Brother, XII's teachings affected readers emotionally and psychically. No other Aquarian student was able or willing to articulate this experience; before the Aquarian experiment was over, furthermore, most students and disciples were repeating gossip and generalities as fact. E.A. Lucas was interviewed in 1960, for instance, and though some of his "memories" are of interest, they also contain pure flights of fancy. "A morning now set apart; din and clank of the great city sank back; a casement had opened as if from a continental headland," Lucas intones. "Below us at last was the sea; we felt the Wind. There were quiet realizations."

That's how it was, Comfort was recalling, when he wrote the Introduction to The Brother, XII's *Foundation Letters and Teachings*, published in 1927. He makes it clear that to follow the teachings of

The Brother, XII was to leave the old world and its problems and its teachings behind. To follow this leader was to step into a new world. Little wonder then that most of the "students" took the experiment at Cedar-by-the-Sea so very seriously. Any reader of the Greek poet-novelist Nikos Kazantzakis will understand the extent of the commitment of the students coming to the Aquarian Foundation. Kazantzakis deals with the subjugation that necessarily follows in some detail in his novel *Saint Francis.*

Men like Will Levington Comfort were clearly seeking religious answers to questions that traditional churches had been unable to confront. To mock this craving, a quest that must be considered the basis for much of the 20th-century culture, is a profoundly ignorant gesture. Bruce McKelvie understood this and voiced his thoughts to Alfred Barley in 1932: "For myself, I have my own philosophy; my own ideas founded upon the teachings of Christ, but I never knew of any advancement made by any body of students by treating the honest beliefs of another with ridicule and contempt."

Comfort's name appears next to that of Edward Alexander Lucas's on page four of the Aquarian Foundation's by-laws "dated this 30th day of April A.D. 1927." When I began my research, I judged this Lucas as something of a mystery man, the only Western Canadian to join the Foundation in its earliest days. As far as I know, he never wrote about his time with The Brother, XII, and his few quoted comments suggested to me that his grasp on events at Cedar-by-the-Sea was tenuous. Then Patrick Dunae, of the Provincial Archives of British Columbia found material other researchers had bypassed for one reason or another, and in that new material I learned that Lucas and Comfort were friends and collaborators on a series of articles for The Saturday Evening Post. Lucas did not know exactly what was going on at the Foundation's headquarters, partly because, after October 1928, he had nothing immediate to do with his former associates. Prior to this it is clear from the letters to Mrs. Crawford that Lucas was The Brother, XII's close associate from July 1927 to March 1928--like so many former cultists he was trying to write himself out of the story.

As Brother XII's public reputation grew blacker and blacker, Lucas attempted to put as much distance between himself and the legendary leader as possible. He wanted to be remembered not as a Foundation stalwart or signatory of the by-laws but as Edward Alexander Lucas, a married man with five children, a veteran of World War One, and a Vancouver barrister who had been in practice there since 1909.

Most of the other signatories of the Foundation's by-Laws were U.S. citizens from California and the Midwest. None can be identified today. Wilson, whose occupation is given as "Hd. of the Aquarian Foundation" was then listed as living at 145 4th Street, in Nanaimo.

Documents attached to these by-laws and dated August 18, 1929, identify Wilson as the president, Annie Barley as secretary-treasurer and George F. Hobart as vice-president of the Aquarian Foundation. While we have known Annie Barley from the very beginning of this increasingly complex story, George F. Hobart appears out of nowhere. Further research revealed that he was an elderly druggist from Hamilton, Ontario.

The only other presently traceable name to appear on these papers is that of Robert England. He has already been identified as a former secret service agent, but may only have worked at one time for a private detective agency in the U.S.

These then are the men and women known to have been at Cedar-by-the-Sea during the spring and summer of 1927. It may be true that Oliver G. Hess, a Civil War veteran and lawyer in Missouri, was so taken by the Aquarian Foundation that he wired $10,000 for the cause; if so, I have no documentation to substantiate this.

Several decades later, newspapers would claim that these were "the golden days of the Aquarian Foundation--during 1927 and part of 1928...Money continued to flow in with every mail, and the hotels at Nanaimo could not accommodate all who drove up...to sit at the feet of the teacher."

I had trouble accepting those reports, because I knew that newspapers in the late '20s had failed to report this supposed influx of breathless tourists. I decided it would be worthwhile to take a closer look at the published newspaper accounts of this period.

The first national paper to mention the Aquarian Foundation was Vancouver's *Daily Province*, on October 28, 1928. The B.C. Newspaper Index provided no earlier listing. The article's author was B.A. McKelvie, who was quoting locals as calling the Aquarian Foundation colonists a "harmless lot of faddists" and good spenders in the local stores. Edward Arthur Wilson is identified in the piece as a retired sea captain. The Foundation, claimed McKelvie, had two thousand members in Canada and the United States, not the eight thousand later mentioned. The only recorded comment by one of the founders on this membership figure came from Alfred Barley late in 1932; at that point, he spoke of a number of people in New Zealand, Africa and England who were continuing to show interest in the Foundation's work.

"No more idealistic location for a settlement could well be imagined than that of the Aquarian Foundation at Cedar," McKelvie's article continues. "The land, consisting of two hundred acres of pleasant groves and delightful copses, [is] exquisite at this time in the florid colorings of autumn."

There were "eight or ten" houses on the site, he writes, and all but two represented investments of $8,000 to $15,000. One house, built by a man no longer resident, had its own electrical system, gardens, garages "and other magnificences." That one was known at the time of McKelvie's visit in 1928 as "the guest house." Maurice Von Platen was described to McKelvie as "the man with the money," and his home as the most expensive--"must have cost at least $15,000."

A Scotsman identified merely as Cameron was the only person in the Aquarian Foundation's office building the day McKelvie visited. Near the waterfront, Perry H. More and James Janey Lippincott were at home in their small house. Perry More was deemed to be "a most agreeable little bearded man, whose whole heart and soul are wrapped up in his beliefs," and Lippincott commented to McKelvie that he had formerly been a draftsman in Los Angeles but was now designing astrological charts.

The man "no longer resident" was Philip J. Fisher, who is still thought by some to have been the son of the late John Arbuthnot Fisher, Admiral of the Fleet. Interesting as this tidbit first seems, it's hardly possible: the elder Fisher was "succeeded in the peerage by his only son, Cecil Vavasseur, who was born in 1868."

"E.A. Wilson, 'Brother XII,'" continued McKelvie, was "a spare, slightly stoop-shouldered, pale-faced and aesthetic-looking man, who sports a thick, square-cut greying beard." Though McKelvie thought him between fifty-five and sixty years old, he was actually just fifty in 1928.

Years later (on January 8, 1960) the retired Vancouver barrister E.A. Lucas remembered several of the people at Cedar in the earliest days. Annie Barley was a crank of the first water, he said, "an old bitch"; Alma Wilson was, he said, an old biddy who looked like a reformed witch and floated about quite unaware of what was going on, and someone he called Sprey-Smith was "one of the world's god damn fools." Fred Pope, he added, was a frail young man who wanted to escape and finally did. A 1929 directory I checked identifies Sprey-Smith as a retired captain and Pope as a cook. According to Lucas in the 1960 interview, both men had travelled from England with The Brother, XII. Fisher, Lucas continued, had gone crazy in 1927 and "wandered about the settlement claiming he was Brother IX."

Wilson at that time, Lucas said, was a man of slim build, about 125 pounds with a "rather effective hesitancy in his speech; after a few words his voice would rasp." He suffered from angina pectoris and took nitroglycerine pills.

From other sources I learned that Coulson Turnbull, described as "the best astrologer on the North American continent," was no longer at the Foundation's headquarters, having already moved to Cornwall Street in Vancouver.

The reason so few people were then at the Foundation was because of the infamous Isis episode. It's implied in an early version of the story that she was one of the "hundreds" of students who had visited during the summer. The people at the Foundation late in October 1928 were speaking darkly of Isis as "the magdalene from Chicago."

She and Wilson often visited one of the islands nearby, a spot for a possible new colony. It was also said that Isis was admitted to Brother XII's secret retreat hidden in a small leafy ravine.

Brother XII, the followers said, had become a different man. "He took the sixth initiation," McKelvie was told, "and he should not have done it. He failed at the test, and his black adept is the cause of it." A couple of the men had even seen this adept. He wore a black cowl that came down to his shoulders. His face, they said, was "like leather that has been smoked for a month."

This black adept was cited as the reason for Brother XII's change. "He is not like that man I knew in California--at all," one man said. They were almost sorry for Brother XII.

Even though I have searched thoroughly, I can find only one bit of documentary evidence to substantiate the Isis-Osiris story. It is clear that something dramatic happened, but the briefest outline is given in one court transcript and no details exist beyond hearsay and gossip. Even E.A. Lucas, who detested Brother XII and what Lucas thought he stood for, had nothing to say about Isis, although in his 1960 interview he did refer to someone else telling him that "Wilson was shacked up with a couple of girls."

It was Lucas and the other deserters who wanted Brother XII's head--and that is why The Brother, XII found himself in court.

V

Their Day In Court

The Isis indiscretions and the breakaway group of Aquarian Foundation members wanting Brother XII's head should be leading us directly to the famous 1928 trial--but real life is never that straightforward.

The popular legend of Brother XII tells it this way: once the Foundation's secretary-treasurer, Robert England, decided to go his own way, he blew the financial whistle. The tale continues with the notion that Brother XII had been misusing Foundation funds and Mr. England had laid charges against him. Enraged, the guilty Brother XII then countercharged England with misappropriating $2,800 from the "Aquarian Society in England." These charges and countercharges, so the legend says, led directly to the famous trial that began "on a hot September day in 1928."

To my boggled amazement when I dug again into the court transcript, I found that nothing about this morsel of the legend was true.

We must assume that when the "Aquarian Society" is mentioned the Aquarian Foundation is meant. Now, I muttered to myself, if the original writers can't set proper legal names down accurately, what indication might we have that they'd be able to get anything else right?

Robert England, for example, was never in Britain with The Brother, XII. He joined the Foundation at Cedar-by-the-Sea in 1927. The "trial" everyone still talks about was not one trial but two hearings. Charged with theft by Wilson/Brother XII, England's hearing took place on October 19; Wilson in turn appeared in court on October 30 to answer Robert England's charge of theft. There's nary a hot September day in it. Having stumbled over one after another of these errors, I found it surprising that anything in the public legend managed to come out right. One bit did, though: the year was 1928.

Since the traditional accounts vary and since it is quite evident that none of these trusted "authorities" bothered to sully their research files with the court records at Nanaimo, I will stick to the court reporter's transcript.

A preliminary hearing, Rex vs Robert England, was held at Nanaimo before the police magistrate C.H. Beevor-Potts on Friday, October 19th, A.D. 1928. The official charge was embezzlement. Frank S. Cunliffe, whom we've already met several times, was Wilson's lawyer. Thomas P. Morton represented the defendant, Robert England.

A Mr. Hagell was called as the prosecution's first witness. After identifying himself as a teller for the Canadian Bank of Commerce in Nanaimo, Hagell testified that yes, he knew Robert England, and that he, Hagell, was acquainted with an account in his bank known as the Mandieh Settlement Fund. Hagell further testified that Robert England and Edward Arthur Wilson were the only ones possessing the authority to draw cheques on this account.

Exhibits one and two were cheques. The first, dated October 3 and made out for $2,000, was made out payable to the accused, Robert England, and signed and endorsed by the accused. On the bottom of this cheque, England had written: "In full payment for all interest in A.F." The second cheque was dated October 5 and was made out for $800, again payable to the accused and signed and endorsed by him. This one carried the note: "Payment in full for all interest in Mandieh Settlement." Both were signed by the accused.

According to Hagell, England first attempted to cash similar cheques late in September 1928, saying that he needed the money for "a deal" and that he needed the cash in large bills. As the bank had nothing larger than twenties, England walked out of the bank. On October 5 he returned with the two cheques that became court exhibits one and two, and this time was happy to take twenties.

The accused at the trial opted to ask no questions.

Frank Cunliffe next called Mr. Wilson, who identified himself as Edward Arthur Wilson, a resident of Cedar District and president of the Aquarian Foundation. On being questioned further, he identified himself as the owner of the Mandieh Settlement Fund, monies given to him by someone who had attached no strings to the donation. He said that Robert England was the Foundation's secretary-treasurer, but was employed by Wilson as "a book-keeper and for general clerical work."

Wilson commented that the term "Mandieh" had no particular significance. "It is just a name," he said. He could not remember drawing any cheques on the Mandieh Settlement Fund, but was sure that England had no "legal or financial interest in that account."

Furthermore, he continued, England had resigned from all of his positions; prior to that, his salary from the Aquarian Foundation had been $50 a month. Four letters of resignation became exhibits three through six: "One as Governor of the Aquarian Foundation, another as Secretary-Treasurer, one as Group-Secretary-General of the Aquarian Foundation, and the other as a member of the Aquarian Foundation."

I made a note to myself that England had resigned four days after being charged with theft--not before--and worked out the odds that his disgruntlement with the Foundation caused him to resign from the Foundation. Not a risky bet.

Exhibits seven and eight were receipts, signed by England, for the two cheques and repeating what he had written on each cheque regarding the Aquarian Foundation and the Mandieh Settlement. Wilson testified that the Foundation was under no financial obligations to the accused and that England "had absolutely no interest in the Mandieh Settlement."

Throughout this exchange one cannot help but be impressed by Wilson's precise answers. He wastes no words. An example of his control appears in the following exchange.

Q. [Cunliffe] Did you have any conversation with the accused?

A. [Wilson] Yes.

Q. When?

A. In the afternoon of October 9th. I first asked him what these receipts represented.

Q. Did you know at the time that he had actually drawn the cheques?

A. No. I asked him what they represented and he told me it was money to which he thought he was entitled. I told him he had no legal right to it. He said he had and that he was going to retain it and that he would decide what he would do with it.

Q. Did anything else happen on that occasion?

A. A whole lot of things happened. You had better ask me just what it is you want to know.

The next day England had again refused to hand over the money. On being asked if he had accomplished the Mandieh Settlement business he was to have done in Vancouver, England told Wilson that he should probably go to Vancouver himself if he was so worried about his purchases. The next day, October 11, Wilson was unable to find England and, learning that "he had gone," he "went to the Police Office and told them the facts and had a warrant issued for his arrest."

The defence lawyer then asked Wilson if he knew anything about " a missing diary kept by the accused." Wilson said he did not. Morton asked if he had a copy of the Aquarian Foundation's constitution with him. Wilson didn't, so the lawyer for the accused sat down.

Cunliffe next called Sergeant John Russell, the Provincial Police officer who had phoned the Vancouver police. When the boat from Nanaimo arrived at the Vancouver wharf and England stepped off carrying two "grips" or travelling bags, he was immediately arrested and trotted back to Nanaimo. All this happened on October 11.

And that was that--the unceremonious end of the prosecution's case. The accused had nothing to say and no evidence to call. Magistrate Beevor-Potts committed him "for trial at the next Court of Competent Criminal Jurisdiction for the County of Nanaimo."

It wasn't entirely the end of the discomforts for the accused, however. Another document, signed by Beevor-Potts and dated October 19, makes it clear that England took another boat ride, this time under police guard. He was escorted into Vancouver and onward to Oakalla Prison Farm.

Robert England was soon enough back in action. On October 24, 1928, he filed charges against Edward Arthur Wilson for stealing $13,000 from the Aquarian Foundation, "on or about August 28, 1928." On the same day that charges were laid, Wilson was arrested--and promptly released on $10,000 bail.

The next day, October 25, Robert England charged Wilson again. This time it was for stealing $5,000 from the Aquarian Foundation. A note in Beevor-Potts's handwriting at the bottom of this document suggests nothing further was done about this charge.

A subsequent document regarding Wilson's bail is interesting only in that it tells us that George Hobart and Alfred Barley put up $2,500 each, and that Wilson's own lawyer Frank Cunliffe put up $5,000.

"The transcript of the Proceedings at Preliminary Hearing of Edward Arthur Wilson (Cedar District) Charged with Theft of $13,000.00" holds few surprises for a researcher reading patiently through.

The only new figure, initially, was Victor B. Harrison, later to be Mary Connally's lawyer when she sued The Brother, XII; he was described as a Nanaimo barrister watching the proceedings on behalf of The Honourable Attorney-General.

On the day before this particular hearing, Attorney-General

R.H. Pooley had been petitioned by three of the Aquarian Foundation governors, E.A. Lucas, Robert De Luce and Maurice Von Platen. These men wanted the Foundation dissolved, but Pooley wouldn't interfere until the courts had decided their case.

The only documented account of the Isis-Osiris story appears on page fourteen of the forty-seven page transcript. According to Robert England, Wilson "told me that when travelling from Seattle to Chicago he had met a woman and that they had been together and that they had both taken the 'Sixth Initiation.' He said that he himself was the reincarnation of the ancient Egyptian god named Osiris. The woman was the reincarnation of the goddess Isis. There had been a conception and a son would be born to them who would be the reincarnation of Horus. The object of this settlement on the Island was that the result of the union between the re-incarnation of Osiris and Isis would bring into the world a son who would be the re-incarnation of Horus, who in the year 1975 would be a World leader."

England, throughout his testimony, does not reveal an equally firm grasp of the facts pertaining to his handling of Foundation monies. He often can't remember doing something or writing letters that bear his name, then admitted that he knew Wilson was defrauding the Foundation almost from the beginning. Wilson was the boss, however, and he was scared of Wilson, he said, so he played along until Wilson charged him with theft.

Odds and ends emerge. The Hess trust money is never given a source in the courtroom; as its monies are always discussed as pounds, one must assume that, if it existed, the money was being moved through British and not American banks. Robert England had been involved in accounting work for fifteen years, so he testifies. This makes his "career" as a detective or a secret agent doubtful. When McKelvie met him days prior to the trial he appeared to be a "sunburned young man in his thirties."

In the midst of this trial, so say the legend's published authorities (who are rapidly becoming the authors of an apocryphal text), England's "elderly" lawyer Thomas Morton "suffered a dizzy spell" in mid-trial. He is reputed to have said, as he turned to lawyer Frank Cunliffe, "This is ridiculous but I have completely forgotten what I was saying." The pundits claim that the Foundation members present in the courtroom realized this was evidence of Brother XII's black Egyptian magic.

First things first. Morton could not have been particularly elderly at that 1928 trial since he was still in active practice at

Nanaimo in 1940. There is no reference to the dizzy spell or to the words Morton supposedly uttered to Cunliffe. Nor is there any mention of this now-famous incident in the newspapers reporting the trial.

A pattern emerged rapidly from the questions and answers in the courtroom. Morton and Cunliffe were battling over one issue: did the $23,000 given to The Brother, XII belong to him, as he claimed, or was the money given to the Aquarian Foundation? No one appeared to know for sure.

The Brother, XII had been running his organization pretty well single-handedly. No one knew Mary Connally, who had been the source of the funds. Coulson Turnbull, the probable contact between The Brother, XII and Brother Mary (Mary Connally), was not called to produce evidence, and neither was he in the court. The magistrate thought the developing case should be considered a civil matter, as he saw it as "a difference of opinion between two factions as to which of the two should control the funds." E.A. Lucas, who was on the witness stand as a Governor of the Aquarian Foundation but who was also a practicing lawyer in Vancouver, thought the matter "purely criminal."

Further testimony on November 1 clarified nothing. Things might have stayed put right there until the case was brought up before the "next Court of Competent Criminal Jurisdiction" had not The Brother, XII--who did not testify at all during this hearing-- unexpectedly pulled his financial angel out of the hat.

Mary Connally had raced to the Nanaimo courtroom by train and ship from Nevada. She arrived to make it clear what she considered the situation concerning the money to be, as far as she was involved. Ten thousand dollars was to be "loaned to the Aquarian Foundation," she said, "$8,000 [was] to be put into the new Settlement [the Mandieh Settlement], which was to be a place of refuge, and $5,000 at my own suggestion was to be invested by Mr. Wilson for his own personal use at 6% to be used by him personally in hard times."

After the swirls and curliques of heated uncertainty, Brother Mary's announcement was a bracing blast of cold fresh air.

VI

Shifting Perspectives

About the time I was deep in the Nanaimo court transcripts, I began rereading Josephine Tey's novel, *The Daughter of Time*, and weighed it with new respect.

In the novel, Alan Grant, a hospitalized police detective, researches the story of Richard III's murder of his two nephews in the Tower of London, a deed that has made the murderer's name a synonym for evil. Grant discovers that "Sir Thomas More's history of Richard III...[is] a damned piece of hearsay and a swindle." In response to a friend's question about another authority on Richard III's black deeds, the character Grant replies, "No, it read like a columnist. Like a columnist who got his information below-stairs."

These were sentiments I recognized and relished as day after day I discovered the facts behind Brother XII becoming increasingly bizarre.

Those who were not surprised by the distance between the truth as it emerged from the transcript and the popularly accepted legendary account of the trial will no doubt be equally calm in facing the next few twists in the authorized version of Brother XII's escapades.

Gwen Cash wrote that she'd had dinner with Robert England the night before the trial in Nanaimo. The next day, by her account, he disappeared from the Nanaimo-bound steamer. Returning to the transcript of the hearings, we find that Robert England was a witness (though a very unconvincing one) at not just one but both hearings. Contrary to Gwen Cash's eye-witness account, we know he did not disappear on his way to Nanaimo.

Turning to the newspapers of the day, I found an almost equally garbled account in a "Special to The Province." A front-page story in the November 22, 1928, issue of *The Vancouver Daily Province* excitedly flashed to its readers that "Aquarian Treasurer is missing, Robert England, Ex-officer Fails to Appear at Assizes, Last Seen in Seattle." The writer of this piece did his damndest, this side of the law, to convince his readers that there was something mysterious about this disappearance. Rumour had it that England was afraid to face the court, yet friends claimed (so our writer continued) that England had had no reason to doubt the outcome of the case. This had been borne out by the grand jury, which returned "no bill" to the indictment.

Remember this: Robert England had testified that he'd not only known of Wilson's light-fingered manner with money but that he'd gone along with it from the start. Then The Brother, XII's lawyer had made England look like a fool during the second hearing. The next spin occurred when the two, Cunliffe and his client Wilson, pulled financial angel Connally from their collective hat. This one-two-three would surely have made England more than nervous.

If England had confidants, they've never spoken out about him in any material I am able to track. Chances are, after sixty-one years, we'll never know his side of the story that led up to Wilson's charging him with theft. By the time the second hearing ended, England must have realized he could win only by running.

Here's my revision of England's story based on the facts as we know them today. England, a young and faithful follower of The Brother, XII, was not particularly bright; either that, or he was too unnerved by the revolution he saw building around him to function with good judgement.

The presence of the "magdalene from Chicago" reminded everyone of the charges of immorality that had periodically rocked various theosophical groups. There was the all-too-active and infernally loud Aleister Crowley in England and Europe. Elsewhere charges had been laid against Charles Webster Leadbeater, a criminal or a black magician or a clairvoyant, or one of the greatest of all occultists--take your pick. Opinion aside, he was also a major figure in the theosophical movement, and even though the charges were proven false, the accusations could still put the fear of the Lord into many within the Island group. What they saw coming upset them. The "magdalene's" exact role in the situation is one we'll probably never know; the important thing, really, was that she was the catalyst.

Brother XII's sex life seemed to have upset the lawyer E.A. Lucas. Though he never talks about Isis, he mentioned "girls" in a recorded private conversation, and in court he hints at actions he perceives as immoral. Neither of these comments is damning: we have no inkling what Lucas (father of three daughters) thought moral or immoral.

Brother XII's activities also upset Maurice Von Platen and Robert De Luce. The former was later described by Lucas as "dull but level-headed" and De Luce was then "a theosophist and astrologer" from California. Coulson Turnbull's name is usually associated with these men, as is Will Levington Comfort's. Comfort may have departed earlier than this after a theological dispute with Edward Arthur Wilson; he was, at any rate, something of a butterfly fluttering from one answer to another. Turnbull never spoke out or wrote, so we don't know his opinion of events; all we know for sure is that about this time England disappeared.

What is important, and this is made clear by the interview with Lucas in 1960, is that Lucas and the others had all been friends and associates of Comfort's long before The Brother, XII appeared on the scene. Comfort's departure may have left the others feeling awkward: did they now follow their old friend or The Brother, XII? Whatever happened, could the Isis episode have given them a reason to return to California to rejoin Will Comfort?

England watched the moral and ideological storm-front closing in on Cedar-by-the-Sea, and he grew daily more frightened. He knew there was very little money in the Aquarian kitty, and that if a judge did dissolve the Foundation, those few dollars were going to be split dozens of ways. After thinking about the situation, England may have decided to pay himself what he viewed as "back wages." Perhaps he thought that since Wilson had played fast and loose with Mary Connally's donation, Wilson was either in no position to complain or, foreseeing the doom England anticipated, would not begrudge his faithful accomplice $2,800. The amount was small potatoes compared to the thousands Wilson had siphoned from the Connally donation.

England seriously misjudged both the situation and Wilson. Wilson, it would appear, tried to reason with him, and when England disappeared on the Vancouver-bound steamer, he filed charges. This appears to be a cool and honest response. England subsequently put up no defence in court, thinking, perhaps, that his countercharges would out-bluff Brother XII. But he was to find out that he was holding a pair of twos while Wilson was gripping the aces and kings.

As England had tried to escape once, why shouldn't he jump bail? E.A. Lucas was England's lawyer at the second hearing, and he later told an interviewer that England had told him he'd put the money "in a safety deposit box in Seattle." Lucas "advised him to go to Seattle and bring it back." We know the rest of the story: England was never seen again.

Interestingly, when the commonly-held version of the story

claims that England's disappearance allowed Brother XII to "expel the malcontents," the legend is almost right. His luck was on a roll. England's disappearance made him the victor without having to go to court a second time; Mary Connally had backed his claims; and on November 9 there was yet another victory.

Headlines that day proclaimed "Brother XII wins first court fight." His application to have the injunction removed that enjoined him from dealing with assets and securities of the Foundation or interfering with its business was successful. This injunction, brought by De Luce, Von Platen and Lucas, had, for some days, prevented Brother XII from touching Foundation funds or continuing his Foundation business.

Up to this point, everything brought to court was another battle won by Edward Arthur Wilson/The Brother, XII, and on November 10, he won another one. James J. Lippincott and Perry J. More, whom he'd charged with trespassing, were found guilty before Magistrate Beevor-Potts on the morning of the tenth. Lippincott was fined the minimum sum possible under such a charge, $2.50; this he paid, along with court costs. It was suggested to More that he move his belongings from the Aquarian Foundation's property immediately and appear on the morning of the following Tuesday for sentencing.

On the least read of *The Vancouver Daily Province*'s pages, we find the continuing story of the Aquarian Foundation hidden away under "Application for dissolution" and "Pooley to Hear Aquarian Group." Then comes the stunner. On December 13, 1928, there's this showstopper: "Brother Twelve Launches Suit Against Foes." F.S. Cunliffe, acting under orders from The Brother, XII, had sued the already-identified group of three, plus Coulson Turnbull, for $100,000 damages.

Bluff or not, it worked. On April 23, 1929, the concerned parties agreed to discuss the dissolution of the Aquarian Foundation, but contrary to all legends The Brother, XII remained in control. Abrogation did not take place until November 16, 1929.

Very likely, no one cared. Edward Arthur Wilson and his current lady, Madame Zee, were overseas. Cunliffe was busy with other business. The men and women who were still living and working at the Foundation's headquarters had long before realized they had no need for a charter.

But then comes the matter of the fabulous gold horde Brother XII collected while running the Aquarian Foundation. One internationally known writer claims quite unequivocally that a Foundation carpenter had been asked to build forty-three boxes to hold all the stolen gold and bills of "one and two-dollar denomination." More than once it has been claimed that the carpenter himself testified to this.

In the late 1960s, when I was working on an earlier draft of this book, it was repeatedly claimed that the coins were $20 gold pieces. Robert England or Edward Arthur Wilson had driven to various Nanaimo banks or banks in nearby villages, the stories went, and cashed the money in for gold.

Initially, this sounds reasonable--but the logic faded faster than mist in the sunshine once I started asking questions. Were any of these statements documented? No. Was the gold ever mentioned in the 1928 or 1933 hearings? No. Did any man identified as a carpenter, construction worker or handyman ever testify? No. Did Robert England or anyone else ever mention large sums of money passing through their hands? No. Was any large amount of money mentioned in court that could not be traced directly to Mary Connally? No. Was there any money proven to have been donated to the Aquarian Foundation that was not accounted for? No. This was fast evaporation of the gossip-tales.

"And if there was one word," I read in *The Daughter of Time,* "that a policeman loathed more than another it was hearsay. Especially when applied to evidence." Something twigged; I phoned a Victoria coin dealer. On hearing my puzzlements, he started laughing. First of all, he told me what I already knew--that $430,000 in $20 coins would have amounted to 21,500 individual coins. That isn't an unmanageable quantity, I was thinking to myself--but I didn't see what was coming. Canada, the dealer pointed out, did not mint a $20 coin until 1967. I mentally took a step back, and began again.

If Brother XII had been hoarding Canadian $10 gold coins, it means he must have had about eighteen hundred pounds of coins. That would make each box weigh in at about forty-one pounds. It would also mean he squirreled away forty-three thousand gold pieces. Even if these figures are not to the penny, surely someone would have begun to notice the sheer number of coins being shipped into the Nanaimo area--and then disappearing from circulation. The coin dealer put it much more bluntly: "There has never been a rumour that this amount of gold was moving into that area."

If the coin dealers didn't hear about the gold, if the banks didn't testify about the gold, where was Brother XII getting all these coins? One easy answer, of course, is to say he wasn't receiving thousands of dollars through the mails in 1927 and 1928 at all.

I needed further details on the legendary story of how money rolled in to the Aquarian Foundation. Information began to emerge from recently-located documents that groups of Aquarian Foundation students were formed in places such as Seattle. They bought The Brother, XII's books and pamphlets from Foundation headquarters and each member paid a membership fee of one dollar a month. Except for the donation by Mary Connally and the possible donation by O.G. Hess, for which I find no documentation, there is no record of substantial donations. Any money former members later said they lost to Brother XII was never proven, except by the ever-faithful Alfred and Annie Barley and by Mary Connally.

One occupational hazard of the seasoned sleuth is that you ask a question and the tall tales fade into the rainforest or the woodwork, depending on your surroundings. After a fair amount of work, I knew less about The Brother, XII, or Brother XII, or Edward Arthur Wilson--call him what you will--than a diligent reporter might have discovered early in April 1927.

The documents in the case are few and far between. All the witnesses are dead. The lawyers and judges, the policemen are dead. The one exception is Cecil Clark, one of the first Provincial Police officers to visit the Aquarian Foundation's property. Documenting The Brother, XII's story has become nearly impossible.

If the trials were hearings, if the first trial was actually two hearings, if the accused was actually the prosecuting party, if the loser seems to have won all his battles and if the famous gold did not exist--who was Edward Arthur Wilson? What can we now tweeze out as truth about him, as a man, a breathing and thinking human being?

The mysteries surrounding him continue. Only recently, a person doing some work for me in England swore that in one government archive he found the file that contained Edward Arthur Wilson's last will and testament. On opening it he found it--empty.

VII

Madame Zura De Valdes

In this business, treasures occasionally appear unheralded in the mailbox. In response to one of reporter Bruce McKelvie's sporadic articles on Brother XII in *The Vancouver Daily Province,* a man wrote him a letter. Dated July 18th, 1939, it opened up a whole new vista.

"I knew Wilson and his wife Mabel as Skottowe during the years 1912 to 1919," the letter said. "He was employed as bank teller in the branch of the 'Union Bank of Canada' at Lancer, Sask., and with only a short period of about 3 yrs service with the bank was appointed manager at a new branch being opened at Portreeve the next town to Lancer. He was smart alright and bragged he had been a sailor, cow-puncher and what not.

"Mabel, whose maiden name was Rowbotham, joined her parents at Lemsford next town west of Portreeve about 1912, and I believe it was the following year she was appointed teacher at the Lemsford Consolidated School, and taught about 2 years when she married Skottowe as he called himself, about this time he was appointed Manager of the new branch at Portreeve, which after 3 or 4 years was closed down and Skottowe discharged owing to a great number of bad loans he made.

"His method of letting out loans was as follows. He got a loan company agent to drive out with him and get farmers to take out a mortgage on their farms. Then Skottowe would advance a loan from his bank of 50% of mortgage and get a rake off of 10% divided between Skottowe and the loan agent. In many cases [the] loan company refused to accept a mortgage, and thus Skottowe was left with a bank loan he could not recover."

The letter-writer, who gave his address as 1195 Cortell Street, Capilano P.O., North Vancouver, went on to say that, "Skottowe and his wife Mabel moved to Vancouver and nothing more was heard of them till some 6 or 8 yrs (I am not quite sure what year) ago." It was then that he was given a clipping "giving details of the charges and their escape by boat." In this report of the case, Mabel's maiden name was given as well as the name "de Valdes."

Although there is no reason to believe this letter to be some sort of pointless hoax, taking it seriously in all its details would be just as pointless. Mabel and Skottowe were certainly married and living in Portreeve, as the man claims. That it was the same woman, there can be little doubt. But there is no reason at this point to connect this man Skottowe, whose first name is not given in the letter, with Edward Arthur Wilson.

We know from information recently found in the records of the American Theosophical Society that Edward Arthur Wilson was living in California and Tahiti during the years Skottowe was working in Saskatchewan. Wilson, with his obvious nautical knowledge and his background in theosophy, can step into The Brother, XII's shadow without disturbing anything. All that the Skottowe persona could do would be to reinforce the supposedly criminal depths of the legend's silhouette.

Although the letter-writer gave his address and phone number, it does not appear that McKelvie contacted him. In what seems to be a response to the information in this letter (passed on to Alfred Barley by Harrison & McIntyre, Victor Harrison's Nanaimo law firm), Barley writes: "In reply to your letter of August 4...I have no direct personal knowledge of the matter and can only say that the statement surprised me very much, and I should not be disposed to consider it correct."

What he says next is the only recorded statement by an intimate concerning Wilson's background: "When I first saw him at Southampton in January 1927, he was living with a lady understood to be his wife, and who was certainly not Mabel Skottowe. This lady came to Nanaimo from England at the same time that we did and by the same boat, stayed at the same house in Northfield, and later came with him to the house next to ours at Cedar. She was always addressed and spoken of as Mrs. Wilson unless by her Christian name, Elma (domestic contraction for Ellen May I think); though there are I believe grounds for supposing that he was not formally or legally married to her."

All of this has been more or less expected up to now. Alfred Barley concludes his all-too-brief excursion into the past with an unexpected glimpse into Wilson's relationship with Elma or Alma, as she most often has been known: "He certainly treated her with great consideration, and even forbearance, during my knowledge of them." Has Barley forgotten that Alma left Wilson and the Aquarian Foundation because of Isis, "the magdalene from Chicago?" Is he covering up? Or, perish the thought, maybe she did not leave for that reason at all?

What he goes on to say about Wilson fits what we now know like a glove: "As regards E.A.W. I have grounds for believing that he was born in Birmingham [Edgbaston?] in the late 70's [1878], his father being, I understand, a clergyman--Rev. Thomas Wilson--of the sect known as 'Irvingites'."

This information is confirmed by the data on the Swiss death certificate. There is no point in thinking that Wilson and Skottowe were the same person --although Skottowe may have been buried in Wilson's place. I'll return to that intriguing point in due course.

In an earlier chapter dealing with Madame Zura, I identified her as Mabel Skottowe, and quoted Gwen Cash's report that her husband's name was Julian Churton Skottowe. According to our interpretation of the Authorized Gossip Version, Mabel reached Cedar-by-the-Sea with Roger Painter from Florida sometime in 1929.

Barley's memory reinforces this reading to some extent: "Since you ask for indirect information I give the following as hearsay that I consider reliable. That she [Mabel] was married in Canada to a Mr. Skottowe who was a Manager of a branch Bank somewhere in Canada. That this Mr. Skottowe's father was a minister in Pensacola, Florida (1926-29). That she had left her husband while they were residing in Seattle, Wash., approximately in 1925 or 1926, where he also worked in a Bank at that time, and that when she left her husband in Seattle, she visited her husband's father in Pensacola. That she never met the man called E.A.W. until she went to Canada in 1929 or 1928. (This I firmly believe)."

This statement is just different enough from the legendary version to make the reader remember that Leona Painter testified in the hearing in 1933. What did she have to say about Mabel Skottowe, their fellow traveller from Florida? According to Leona Painter, she and her husband reached Cedar-by-the-Sea for the first time in 1930; the de Valdes couple "were away in England at this time."

So Mabel wasn't brought to the Foundation's colony by Painter. Bruce and Georgina Crawford were also from Florida, and they testified at the 1933 hearing. Nothing is gained from turning to them, however, since they'd not known Mabel Skottowe in Florida. There are no other clues.

The North Vancouver letter writer said that he had known the Skottowes through until 1919. This proves Julian had not died overseas in World War One, and the military records verify it. As the letter-writer quoted earlier had known Mabel for years and knew her family as well, she was probably Canadian; from 1913 through 1915 Mabel Rowbotham was apparently a school teacher at the Lemsford Consolidated School in Lemsford near Portreeve.

It is criminal that no one has tried to track her down through her family; for all I know she may be a 90-ish dowager living in Saskatchewan, and I have not been able to find her. There are no other leads into the background of the woman who became Zura de Valdes in 1931.

Two situations emerge as valuable puzzle-pieces from the testimony in the 1933 hearing. The first is that Madame Zura appears to have lived at Cedar-by-the-Sea only briefly before she and her consort departed for England, and her reign of terror--the cracking whip, the drug-crazed behaviour--began only on her return and, even then, not immediately.

The second piece of the puzzle that came out of the 1933 testimony concerns money. Before proceeding, let's flash back. Toward the end of that long letter written to Bruce McKelvie in July 1939 we find what may be the first glimmer of the jars-of-gold story. "I lived," he writes, "on Gabriola Island for 1 year Sept 1937 to Sept 1938 and herd [sic] a lot of this religious sect [Aquarian Foundation], [which] it appears cached hundreds of quart jars of chicken, fruit, etc., on Gabriola Island and protected same by armed men on shore, challenging anyone approaching by boat." Not gold but food? Victuals to outlast Armageddon? Mormonesque self-sufficiency? Let the matter rest as a newly opened question.

One way of delving further in another area is to begin to track who was where, when. Sometime late in 1928 or early in 1929 Mabel Skottowe showed up at Cedar-by-the-Sea. Beyond this we know nothing. What led The Brother, XII to choose her from among many others there is as much a mystery today as it was to the Aquarians sixty years ago. As none of them ever made documentable statements about this period of time, we have no information concerning the couple's trip to England. The legend as written provides no dates. Mary Connally is on record as saying they were away all of 1929 and 1930.

We know they returned on November 14, 1930 because there are newspaper reports to that effect. The couple was in the area early in June 1929, because it's known that Ada G. Phillips was interviewed in the Malaspina Hotel by Wilson on June 6, 1929. But after that? We don't even know where they were.

Questions lead to other questions. Alfred Barley was put in charge of the business end of Aquarian affairs, and Roger Painter was made spiritual leader. It was to Painter that Brother XII wrote the "kooky" letters that caused Painter to fear for his leader's sanity yet, according to his wife's testimony in 1933, they did not even meet Brother XII until his return in November 1930.

During the absence of the de Valdes couple, Leona and Roger Painter (according to Leona's courtroom testimony, which went undisputed) lived in the de Valdes home, and their task was to look after the De Courcy Island property. Leona mentions a letter, one written to her and her husband by Zura de Valdes concerning the money Mary Connally had given to Wilson and what they had done with the money. Leona Painter could not produce the letter, as it had "mysteriously disappeared."

It is quite feasible that if Mary Connally had not given The Brother, XII that $23,000, the Aquarian Foundation would not have stirred a ripple beyond its own borders. The gift of that money is one plain and clear documented fact that emerges from an investigation of the legend of Brother XII.

Sometime during these few months, Myrtle Baumgartner is said to have had a miscarriage, or two miscarriages, or was delivered of a baby girl, or had a nervous breakdown. Which was it? Mary Connally never mentioned Myrtle by name when she testified in court in 1933, but it is known that Mary Connally nursed her back to health in Vancouver during the winter of 1928 and then, according to Annie Barley, took her east. Emerging from this testimony are several unreported facts. Myrtle Baumgartner, for instance, told Mary Connally her real name was "Jenner"; another woman thought this Myrtle was from Toronto; while a third, Ada G. Phillips, got a real earful. The Brother, XII had read to Ada Phillips a letter from "Myrtle 'Bout'" and then described her as his "soulmate" who had gone insane and was now writing letters to her "Osiris" begging for money. He admitted sending her $250.

This statement from Ada Phillips reminded me of the comments Brother XII had earlier made to Robert England about Isis and the Sixth Initiation. Wilson was a reticent man whose closest associates (the Barleys and E.A. Lucas) knew little of his personal life, yet employees (England) and strangers (Painter) and interviewees (Phillips) are the people to whom he spoke intimately.

I suddenly realized that Brother XII's story could now be reduced to a few pages. Luckily, at this point, I discovered a new lead.

James A. Santucci is the only scholar to write about The Aquarian Foundation. In the conclusion to his professorial paper he makes a number of telling points, even though as he wrote he was following the popularized legend. That public lore, he admits, considers

Wilson "a complete fraud who duped many who should have known better." Though Santucci had no way to break through the fog of gossip and lies, to his eternal credit he doesn't quite believe the story.

"Wilson," Santucci wrote, "had the requisite knowledge (a theosophical substructure and astrological superstructure), the ability to communicate that knowledge, and the charisma to create an effective and sustaining messianic myth to retain and sustain his disciples."

Santucci's comments on the disciples reminded me that one aspect not yet considered was the age of Wilson's followers. For the most part, they were a generation older than the age of the typical follower or groupie. Cults are for the young.

What else went wrong? Strife had followed the Isis embarrassment, and three governors had attempted to overthrow Wilson. Perhaps the Foundation had been weakened beyond repair, and Wilson never quite got his feet under him again.

These are all keys to the Foundation's failure but, more important (and complex in its ramifications) is the already-discussed period between the departure of the angry and frightened colonists from De Courcy Island in their rowboat and the moment the Barleys and Mary Connally, with Victor Harrison's help, filed charges against The Brother, XII.

VIII

The Gurdjieff Experiment

Reading between the lines of documents sixty years old is all too easy, and what we conjure in imagination, all too convincing. History, we figure, is at our whimsical command. Who can resist the urge to step backwards and change things to the way they could or should have been? To varying degrees everyone who writes or talks about the past alters it slightly, and whether that's for better or worse, I'm not about to judge.

We can say in all good conscience that almost no one set out to paint The Brother, XII with such a heavy black brush. If the background he claimed is true, Wilson was accustomed to command, used to standing on the bridge giving orders that could not be questioned. The farmers and storekeepers, the small-town lawyers he dealt with on Vancouver Island did not understand this, could not understand his worldview or his religion, and thus tended to resent his ways as tyrannical or worse.

It remains a moot point whether or not anyone was delighted to see things go wrong for him. His attitude, demeanor, beliefs and distant manner made him an unsympathetic character. While alive and able to fight he proved repeatedly that he needed no one to help him fight his battles. Once he'd disappeared and after he had died, the crows and magpies cawed and feasted whence the wolves had once fled, tails between their legs.

This is not the place for a retelling of the theosophical movement worldwide, but it helps to understand the larger picture into which this one small story fits. Suffice it to say that what happened at Cedar-by-the-Sea-- with the wrangling factions, the immoral actions of a leader, the sordid battle for financial control-- was merely a miniscule repetition of what was occurring elsewhere within the movement, as well as being a reflection of previous situations. As in all religions or cults, the Aquarian Foundation's membership was all-too-human.

Even as early as January 1927 the sides were moving into position. In the earliest days of his teachings, months before the founding members of the Foundation caught their ship for Canada, Wilson was attracting attention in print.

The February 1927 number of *The Canadian Theosophist*, under the title "The Sappers and Miners," reported an anonymous writer's attack on the very heart and core of the Theosophical Society. *"The Haldimand-Julius Monthly,"* it read, "contains two articles of immediate interest to members of The Theosophical Society. Their titles indicate the tone and matter of their contents--'Katherine Tingley, Boob-Baiter of San Diego,' and 'Messiahs Made to Order'."

Katherine Tingley was married to one of the assistants to a cofounder (with H.P. Blavatsky) of the Theosophical movement. In 1898, Tingley founded the Universal Brotherhood and Theosophical Society, and for many years the headquarters was at its colony at Point Loma, California.

The second article was an indirect attack on Annie Besant, the president from 1907 to 1933 of the original Theosophical Society founded by Madame Blavatsky. Besant was also a noted Indian political leader.

In its own way the attack reported in *The Canadian Theosophist* was like a Christian attacking Moses and Christ but, as most religious leaders discover to their discomfort, it is a less-than-holy world. The Brother, XII, whose name is brought in about halfway through the article, fares very well indeed.

"Still another story has to be told, although but an indication of it can be given here. Brother XII, who has been writing letters about a new Movement to save the world, and has published a little book, *The Three Truths*, founded on the famous sentences from *The Idyll of the White Lotus*, which is one of the best of these little books which we have read for a long time, and much superior, for instance to *At the Feet of the Master*, has announced his intention of coming to Canada. Literary merit has nothing to do with ethical virtue or we might have taken Lord Byron for an angel and Oscar Wilde for a saint. We fear that Brother XII has his foibles too.

"It is not necessary to accuse Brother XII of anything worse than self-delusion, although several warnings have reached us. An official of the Exeter Lodge in England writes: "We note an article by the 'Master's' personal chela. Curious to relate we were interested in the paper which he circulated and tried to get in touch with him, it being stated he lived in Cornwall. We found he had disappeared, having no outward and visible means of support. He is very much wanted. Many letters await him there, in a little out of the way village near Wadebridge."

The public attitude toward The Brother, XII began favourably enough. One correspondent in California writes: "Brother XII's effort is a little more ambitious and plausible than some of the others; he may--probably will--write an acrimonious or sanctimonious reply but further than that will not start anything which may lead to an investigation of his bona fides."

New material flowed into the gaps in the puzzle. "I hope you will not waste too much room in your precious magazine," a Mr. Christmas Humphreys writes, "over Brother XII of the Aquarian Foundation. He is a Mr. ---- of Southampton and wished to join the Buddhist Lodge as Brother XII. Then I pointed out we could not have people joining anonymously, though he could call himself what he liked when he had joined. He replied like a small schoolboy in a huff. His writings contain nothing not contained in every textbook of Theosophy worth the name, while his whole method of working and general behaviour mark him, for most who have contacted him over here, as just one more deluded humbug who delights in setting himself up as specially favoured by the Masters, and privileged to dole out favours to those who stand in sufficient awe of him."

Christmas Humphreys first turned to theosophy after World War One and then to Buddhism, later becoming the founder of the Buddhist Lodge in London. Not much of a thinker, Humphreys served as a conduit for ideas. It was he who turned Alan Watts towards Buddhism (Watts was already involved in theosophy); it would in turn be Watts who served as teacher to thousands of hippies including those who invaded Vancouver Island in the late 1960s and early '70s.

Although the passages from *The Canadian Theosophist* are long, it is worth quoting them in full because they encompass the seeds of all the problems The Brother, XII was to face at Cedar-by-the-Sea. The difference between Wilson and most of these "humbugs" was his social message, something his critics continually missed or downplayed. There would not be any cataclysmic encounter with the constellation Aquarius as he was said to have claimed, but there would be an Armageddon from which would emerge, circa 1975, a Christ-like leader.

Pretty harmless stuff, this, and in no way original. The Irvingites, the sect in which Edward Arthur Wilson appears to have been raised and wherein his father was a minister, believed "that the

Christian world was not to pass insensibly into the millenial, but was to be terminated by judgements, ending in the destruction of the Church as it then visibly existed, the restoration of the Jews to their own land, and the second coming of Christ; and that the second coming would not be long delayed."

In the proverbial nutshell, there's the kernel of The Brother, XII's vision: death and resurrection, to be symbolic, that could be observed from the peaceful solitude of Cedar-by-the-Sea. This is what was supposed to have happened, but Life got in the way.

Financial problems, like their sexual counterparts, appear to be endemic to cults. The many-times-told story of Aimee Semple McPherson and her Four-Square Gospel Church is not very different from that of The Brother, XII and the Aquarian Foundation. The result of her work, however, was much different; her story is writ large. She was successful, as The Brother, XII was not.

The Brother, XII might have survived these problems, but one he could not overcome was age. Followers in cults are usually fairly young men and women, people with energy and a desire to change their way of life. The one theme running through all the testimony regarding the Aquarian Foundation is that its members were trying to escape the problems of the 20th century and return to the values they'd known as children.

The Brother, XII quite obviously had no intellectual equals in the Foundation, and none of his followers seemed to share his view that the aim of the Foundation was development and growth. Most could not, or would not, understand that The Brother, XII's ideas were continuing to evolve. Their own minds, like the orientation of their testimony in 1933, returned to what their leader had written in 1927 and 1928. As *Unsigned Letters* in 1930 proves, The Brother, XII was moving into a very different spiritual landscape.

"These letters," their author declares, "were written during the period January to December 1929." During at least half of this period, The Brother, XII was supposedly in England fleecing new lambs and buying the *Lady Royal* with money some rich and simple-minded woman had forked over.

That version for some reason never strikes anyone as illogical. But I began wondering--since he had thousands of dollars in gold, why didn't he purchase the ship with his own money? Why did he need a generous woman donor? And if he were so greedy, why (as legend has it) did he hand his gold hoard over for the Barleys to manage while he sailed off for sixteen months? If this story is correct, Brother XII was not only trusting but downright stupid, and he would be called neither by the very people who created the woven myths.

The '60s revival of all manner of things occult fed voraciously on the reaction against the harsh absurdities of self-conscious modern science. It was a turning-away from strident insistence that the universe is purposeless, that evolution is chance, that man is animal or a blind bundle of reflexes. One of the thinkers central to the occult revival of the 1960s and still much-read today, is a Russian-Greek known in history and literature as Gurdjieff. He was an almost exact contemporary of The Brother, XII, and though he was immensely better known and has been extensively written about, we know no more about him personally than we do Edward Arthur Wilson.

Central to Gurdjieff's thinking was mankind's robot-like existence, regardless of social station.

> *The King in a carriage may ride,*
> *And the Beggar may crawl at his side;*
> *But in the general race,*
> *They are traveling all the same pace.*

One of Gurdjieff's methods of freeing man from this self-made prison was a series of highly complicated and physically demanding dances. According to Colin Wilson, a British authority on the occult, Gurdjieff "believed in keeping his students in a perpetual state of intense alertness." This included waking them at four in the morning and demanding that they be performing some complicated aspect of a dance within seconds. He would put them in embarrassing public situations to force them to learn to deal with the extraordinary. He took them on fast and exhausting drives, told long and pointless stories and made it almost impossible for anyone to see him personally unless he himself so wished.

Besides everything else, Gurdjieff apparently possessed a terrible temper and was secretive to an unusual degree. And he was brutal; it is thought that his treatment of the short-story writer Katherine Mansfield led directly to her death. Thousands of students nonetheless believe in his teachings today, and his books and the dozens about him remain in print. During the time he ran his school in France, he attracted such diverse personalities as the American architect Frank Lloyd Wright and the English novelist D.H. Lawrence.

Another who may well have been drawn to Gurdjieff was Edward Arthur Wilson. That Wilson knew of Gurdjieff cannot be doubted. On page 23 of *Unsigned Letters* he quotes from *Tertium Organum*, a book by Russian-born philosopher and thinker Peter Ouspensky. Ouspensky was Gurdjieff's most famous disciple and carried his master's teachings to England. There is not one action or thought revealed by Wilson/The Brother, XII (who was thought to be so "kooky" or "tyranical" or "insane" by a generation or two of Canadian journalists) that cannot be traced directly to the teachings of Gurdjieff.

A self-proclaimed authority on Brother XII recently maintained that the man was a Buddhist. Not only does this hint at ignorance of human nature and an abysmal misunderstanding of 20th-century literature and thought, it unfortunately perpetuates the skewed legend. At the end of his time on Vancouver Island, Wilson/The Brother, XII was still groping in the ontological dark. He had been a Christian, had studied Buddhism (there is an intimate and long-standing connection between Theosophy and Buddhism), was a believer in what was being taught by H.P. Blavatsky and was, with Gurdjieff, moving to new spiritual planes. Edward Arthur Wilson was becoming a quintessential 20th-century "seeker."

The Brother, XII returned from Europe aboard the *Lady Royal* with a developing philosophy in mind and tried to bring it to life at Cedar-by-the-Sea. Work, one of the most immediate ways to break the trap of aimlessness, was his first preoccupation. Gurdjieff had worked his followers to the bone until (to give but one example) a man who could not have mown a lawn when he began studying with Gurdjieff was later mowing acres daily.

No evidence exists to prove that the so-called survivors of the Aquarian Foundation ever read, much less understood, the directions outlined in *Unsigned Letters.* Everything he can be proven to have done until the day his followers "revolted" and (so many months later) sought the help of McKelvie and Victor Harrison is foreshadowed in *Unsigned Letters,* published three years before his followers' court case.

Wilson was doing exactly what he'd seen, or learned of, Gurdjieff doing in France. His mistake was trying to duplicate the drama with elderly spinsters, aged widows, middle-aged and retired astrologers and at least one half-wit.

IX

Cunliffe for the Defense

If it were just a matter of a dramatic vision that went awry, why did The Brother, XII run? Why sink the *Lady Royal* and his other boats? Why inflict so much damage to the Aquarian Foundation's property on De Courcy Island? Those would be the actions of a guilty man--not the innocent man I am claiming I found trapped in shadows of unfounded legend.

Though I have dug I cannot provide documents to answer these and other questions that come to mind. I can, however, think about them in the light of what is known conclusively.

Edward Arthur Wilson-Amiel de Valdes was fifty-four in April 1933, but he looked at least ten years older. He was known to have heart problems and might have had one or more heart attacks while on Vancouver Island; he was physically small, if not frail, by that time. Zura de Valdes was probably in her forties, as we know she married Skottowe about 1915.

Although it has occasionally been said that they had accomplices in their destructive rampage on De Courcy and Valdes Island, the names of any accomplices have never been provided. I had to assume that one unwell man and one middle-aged woman did the woeful damage themselves.

According to an October 29, 1932 letter from Alfred Barley to Bruce McKelvie, the de Valdes couple had already left De Courcy Island. "I hope," it read, "your paper will arrange for you to be present at the trial; (which Amiel de Valdes and Zura de Valdes apparently will not be for they have left De Courcy, and a Registered Letter sent to the young man who was their most devoted servant, has been returned through the mail endorsed 'removed: no forwarding address'.)"

Court documents place them in Rooms 1-3 in the Imperial Building in Nanaimo throughout most of February 1933; this is their last known address. February 25 of that year, when Amiel de Valdes submitted a Statement of Defence through his lawyer, is the last date the couple can be "documented" as being in the Nanaimo area.

Alfred Barley did an on-site inventory of the damage done to Aquarian Foundation property on De Courcy and Valdes islands on April 12, 1933. His report is convincing. Eight days later, on April 20, the court issued an order appointing "William Burnip and George Henry Green, both of the City of Nanaimo, to enter upon the lands in question in this action, being the De Courcy Islands and the lands at Valdes Island, for the purpose of preventing any persons from trespassing upon said lands and from destroying or removing any of the buildings, fixtures and chattels situate thereon."

The intriguing factor about all of this is that, first, Brother XII is not identified as the vandal and that, second, the newspapers do not pick up the story until after the trial. "Aquarian Farms show Appalling Work of Vandals" belatedly screamed the *Daily Colonist* on April 29, 1933. The *Nanaimo Daily Free Press* blandly rehashed the same story later that day. The writer of this twice-chewed piece describes Brother XII's position within the Foundation and goes on to discuss the terrible vandalism and the extent of the damage, but nowhere in this account is Brother XII himself accused of having done the dirty work.

Local and Island papers showed little interest in Cedar-by-the-Sea after that late-April account of the vandalism. A piece appeared a month later on "Brother XII's Rifle Pits"; in June 1933 there was an announcement that "Brother XII's Equipment [is] Sold"; five years later in 1938 a report was published saying that the Foundation no longer existed; and yet another year later, "Finis Written to Long Search for Man of Mystery" records Wilson's only-then-discovered death. A speech about Brother XII was given in 1943 to a local Lion's Club. In 1951, the *Daily Colonist* reported that the *Lady Royal* had become a tuna ship. The coverage was hardly feverish.

Except for obscure comments made by Mary Connally at her court hearing, no one at the time was documented as accusing The Brother, XII of vandalism. In reply to the question of who had left the Aquarian property in "desolation," she replied: "The defendants left it; and more than that, they sold all the things that we had bought with [the] people's money. They sold four thousand jars of canned goods that these people worked day and night to put up. They have done all that since this suit was started."

I'll never know for sure now if Connally's accusation was based on first-hand knowledge or second-hand gossip. She wasn't cross-examined on this point, and it was never brought up again for discussion. Returning to Alfred Barley's inventory of the on-site damage, I discovered that the actual vandalism was slight. Theft had been the far greater problem.

Barley found "no one there. Following is a list of the items of wanton and malicious damage done....Practically nothing was left--everything likely to be useful having been taken away."

1. De Courcy Farm. Windows on ground floor of farm house deliberately broken. Also one or two in the skylights.
2. Water tanks here, deliberately pierced in two places, with axe.
3. Storehouse emptied and door left open.
4. Fruit Trees planted by Edgar Conrow, near barn, all re moved.
5. Bales of wiring (Fencing, etc.) near horse barn, had been removed.
6. All walnut trees (about fifty) gone from near cabin.
7. Mowing machine gone.
8. Seed-cleaning machine gone.
9. Root slicer gone.
10. Cultivator gone.

Among the other "items" gone were two horses, an unknown number of chickens, most of a sawmill, individual windows and doors, a dragsaw and just about everything else that could be moved. It's interesting to note that the items gone were things that farmers and settlers could use. If Brother XII is to be held accountable for this "vandalism," it is quite apparent that he'd had the help of several strong men. He and Zura de Valdes could not have moved heavy equipment and live trees off the island by themselves, for such a feat would have been physically impossible.

Did they sell various items to local people, I wondered, who then moved the goods off the island? Did the locals loot the farms knowing that The Brother, XII was gone and that his followers were huddled at Cedar-by-the-Sea? Either scenario is possible, though the second one has a ring of actuality about it. Nowhere had I found signs that Wilson/The Brother, XII was vindictive--but he could move fast when he wanted to. This transition period is a mysterious blank in which the only gleam of light is the record of Myrtle Skottowe and Edward Arthur Wilson changing their names by deed poll.

Then they disappeared. There was no hint that he had gone upcoast; so far as anyone knew in the early and mid-1930s, he and Zee simply disappeared. Only much later was it told around that the de Valdes couple spent the summer on the coast aboard their tugboat. Not surprisingly, the B.C. Provincial Police officer who supposedly visited them is never named and is never quoted directly. He became another in the growing line of anonymous witnesses: the man who recognized Wilson as a fellow he'd worked with in Victoria, for instance, the unidentified electrician who set up the elaborate microphone system, and the men who saw him studying aboard ship after he'd left Victoria.

The matter went quiet for a time--and then came a stunner. In the "Legals" column of a Vancouver newspaper, the following curious notice appeared.

Julian Churton Skottowe Otherwise Edward Arthur Wilson, otherwise Amiel De Valdes, deceased.

Pursuant to an order of the Chancery Division of the High Court of Justice, dated the twenty-fourth day of April 1939, and made in an action in the matter of the Estate of Julian Churton Skottowe, deceased, William Ewart Craigen against Margery Wilson (widow) 1939 S. No. 340 the creditors of Julian Churton Skottowe...late of Cowley Lodge, Kentsbury, near Blackmore Gate, in the County of Devon, formerly of Portmadoc in the County of Carnarvon and of Nanaimo Island, British Columbia...

And so forth. Local newspapers claimed the death was that of the infamous Brother XII, whom most of their readers had either forgotten or never known. Dr. Donald H. Clark, the first outsider to gather material for a book on Wilson, has written next to the clipping, "The veracity of this death is doubted by many who knew Bro. XII."

Except for his brother's peculiar biography, which tells of Wilson dying in Australia, there has been no plausible alternative to Wilson's recorded death in Neuchatel, Switzerland, on November 7, 1934.

I had been entangled in the death notices when the strangest document in this entire story emerged in the research. It was a letter written by the late Donald M. Cunliffe, Cunliffe & Cunliffe letterhead, to Don Clark. The son of F.S. (Frank) Cunliffe was breaking family silence and writing to the son of Dr. Clark; Clark senior had been the man who'd taken over writing the story of Brother XII from newspaperman Bruce McKelvie. The date of the letter, from which I cannot quote directly because of legal restrictions, is February 12, 1974.

The younger Cunliffe reported to the younger Clark that he had examined the documents in his possession and had found nothing "in writing to dispute" the fact Wilson died on November 7, 1934. In the next paragraph he alludes to "incidents" when he was "a young lad" and writes that though his "recollection is necessarily hazy" it can be "bolstered" by concurrent incidents. Late in June 1936, F.S. Cunliffe had received a phone call that sent him hurrying off to see "Lady Mary"--Mary Connally--at Cedar. The young Cunliffe, the lad Donald, accompanied his father and remembered that he was given a puzzle to work and that the tone of the conversation he overheard between the two adults was "urgent." He remembered that the weather was hot outside and it was stuffy inside the house. The word "brother" was mentioned, he wrote, as were sailing schedules and San Francisco. At one point Cunliffe's father stood up and said, in effect, that he must go to San Francisco to meet "him" and it might be better if he took his family along.

Donald Cunliffe continues in his letter to Clark that he was sure the year was 1936, for after the trip (during which his sister had driven for the first time legally) his father bought a new car, a 1937 Buick. In San Francisco they had stayed at a hotel called either the St. Francis or the Sir Francis Drake. Cunliffe remembers his father in the hotel phoning attorneys in the city, and one shipping line. The next day they visited a bank and spoke to a lawyer there; next, they visited another bank where the boy watched as his father withdrew a sizeable amount of cash and gave it to another lawyer. After lunch they went down to the docks and boarded a liner. The boy was given over to a seaman who proceeded to tour the youngster through the ship, until they were joined on deck by the elder Cunliffe and a man dressed in white. The man was pale and wore a wide-brimmed hat. All the boy heard him say was, "I shan't see you again, Cunliffe, but I may be in touch." The lawyer had said nothing, his son remembered, but looked grim.

Although the older Cunliffe refused ever after to discuss this meeting or the man in white, Donald M. Cunliffe was left with the impression that the man was The Brother, XII, someone his father never wanted to deal with again.

Thirteen months after the June 1936 call, the youngster answered the phone. It was a July Saturday morning in the summer of 1937, and he was getting ready to visit relatives who lived near Smithers. The caller was a transatlantic operator with a Mr. Wilson on the line for F.S. Cunliffe. As he wasn't home, the operator relayed a request: on his return, would Mr. F.S. Cunliffe call the transatlantic operator in Gibraltar.

Donald Cunliffe goes on to say that he knows his father returned the call later that morning, because during the afternoon he took his son down to his office and showed him the Aquarian Foundation's corporate seal. "Keep this after I die," he told his son. "One day it'll be history." He also admitted to his son during this conversation that the caller was the man they had met in San Francisco. And then the senior lawyer swore, something he rarely did.

Beneath this three-page statement to Don Clark is D.M. Cunliffe's name and signature. It's a touching personal document; as I write this I can look up to where, pinned to my wall, is a crisp impression made by the seal that belonged to F.S. and then to D.M. Cunliffe. Their shared story could hardly be one more tall tale. The Cunliffes were not the sort of people to bother to perpetrate nonsense and, forty years after the event, what would be the point?

For every answer emerging in the research there were new questions. If Edward Arthur Wilson had been alive as late as 1937, and he would have been only fifty-nine years old--who was it who had died in Neuchatel, Switzerland on November 7, 1934?

Wilson was also able to draw forth an unexpected amount of loyalty. Only forty years after his disappearance did one of the Cunliffes break the silence about his "disappearance," and neither ever did speak of the details of the specific business with him. Nor did the Barleys ever refute The Brother, XII's early teachings. So, another question: why did they "revolt" and then sue him? I found that answer during an examination of the time between the so-called revolt and the hearings in Nanaimo.

It had all to do with loyalty, all to do with belief. After the legal and emotional trauma she had been through, the elderly and poverty-stricken Mary Connally still murmured with her dying breath she'd give that much again. To the end, her faith in "the old Brother" was unshaken.

Postlude

In writing this book I discovered two things: first, many people don't know the difference between history and fiction and, second, many more don't particularly want to know.

One filmmaker who had been briefly interested in The Brother, XII project made an announcement after our fourth or fifth meeting. "This isn't the story of Brother XII," he insisted. "You people are writing the story of a different man."

To return to the beginning: something happened at Cedar, Cedar-by-the-Sea and Nanaimo--no doubt about that. What it was, that's the real question. I've proven Edward Arthur Wilson was not Brother XII of legend but The Brother, XII of the shadowy and curious world of theosophy and spiritualism--but are we any closer to an answer?

There is no proof that Edward Arthur Wilson/The Brother, XII broke any laws, so it's time we looked elsewhere for the key to this unravelling legend. It can obviously be argued that the last hearings, with the judge finding for the prosecution in both cases, were, in effect, a moral and a legal victory. Be that as it may, the bottom line is that The Brother, XII put up no fight, and nothing of what Mary Connally and her nine witnesses said was proven true.

But notice: the victors had taken home their spoils precisely because their opponent put up no fight.

The more I thought about their 'victory,' the more I felt that within it somewhere lay the final chapter of The Brother, XII's story. The de Valdes couple were gone, for instance, from an unknown date in 1929 (and no great trust should be put in Ada G. Phillips's testimony as to when she'd seen Wilson) to mid-November, 1930. According to Mary Connally the "revolt" took place on March 17, 1931. All the parties went to court two years later in April 1933. Yes, yes, but . . .

I have found no record of anyone seeing The Brother, XII and Zura de Valdes in British Columbia after the "revolt." The fact that they had an address in Nanaimo proves nothing; none of the legal documents in the case bears their signatures; and the stories about them being ensconced in the Empress Hotel in Victoria, and later up-Island, are just that--stories.

Why would a man who seems to have been highly active and intellectually curious (he wrote a book or two a year once he started doing books) be content to sit out on Valdes or De Courcy islands doing nothing? As the character Alan Grant learned in Josephine Tey's *Daughter of Time,* I was finding that what historians claimed to be true in many ways went against commonsense knowledge of human nature. Does anyone really believe that the energized Wilson and his companion lived on the island quietly farming and not going anywhere for two years?

What, then, did happen there? I can't prove it three ways against the middle, but everything points to a plausible reconstruction along the following lines.

The Brother, XII and his lady left the islands soon after the "revolt" early in 1931. Sometime after this, the locals began plundering the buildings and stores on Valdes and De Courcy islands. Cunliffe, hearing about the situation and being a friend of Mary Connally's, urged her to sue The Brother, XII. Otherwise, he might have advised, everything was going to be lost, or (because Harrison was also prodding the others into activity) divided into so many pieces that winning would not matter. Convinced, Lady Mary acted. Broke, she needed the money or property desperately. It's entirely possible the loyal Barleys were party to this plan.

Did F.S. Cunliffe defend The Brother, XII at the latter's request or was he acting on his own? Did Wilson "step from the grave" in 1936 to borrow money from Connally and Cunliffe? Or did The Brother, XII die in Switzerland--and could it have been Zura de Valdes and her husband, Julian Skottowe, an admitted look-alike of Wilson's, who blackmailed Cunliffe and Connally in 1936 and possibly in 1937?

Had Cunliffe acted in Amiel de Valdes's name but without his permission or, at least, without written permission? That put him in a curious position. Skottowe's "reappearance" as Brother XII (and how many outsiders knew what The Brother, XII or Skottowe really looked like?) would have been a crippling blow to Cunliffe. Skottowe may have known a lot, and the record tells us that he wasn't adverse to peculiar dealings. With his wife's help, he could easily have proven that the damage and theft at the Aquarian Foundation's farms on the islands had been caused by locals and not by Wilson.

First off, Cunliffe had acted as a friend of Mary Connally's and had made sure she "won" the case against his "client." Next: he was a blackmailed lawyer who dared not speak up. Finally, Cunliffe was in the role of good citizen who kept the story, along with its ramifications, flat quiet. When his son Donald M. Cunliffe wrote his confessional letter, he may have unknowingly revealed far more than what he had originally seen as a youngster accompanying his father in San Francisco.

Afterword

Acknowledgements

Ladies first. Without the assistance of Mrs. Bruce (Kate) McKelvie and Camilla Newman this book would not exist as you have read it. Jean Kozocari's humour and assistance has been greatly appreciated. Joyce Clark and Rhonda Lillard provided the encouragement that made it possible to stick with the story through thick and thin.

Among the earliest supporters of this book was Art "Ken" Kendall of Boat Harbour. Others have been John Cass, Edward S. "Ted" Henderson, Minard G. (Gerry) Hill, proprietor of Yellow Point Lodge, Victor Harrison, and Donald Cunliffe, who did not live to see this book in print. Thanks are also due Cecil Clark, Willard Ireland, Andy Murdoch, Rex Malthouse, Jim Hume and Alistar MacLeod.

More recently Robin Skelton, Steve Zablosky, Greg Evans, Dennis J. Duffy, David Mason, Christopher Petter, Julian Reid, Barney Hagar, Patrick Dunae and James Santucci have all given freely of their time and information. Thanks also to the staffs of the Provincial Archives of British Columbia and the University of Victoria's McPherson Library.

In no way does their assistance imply that these good people agree with the information and conclusions presented in this book; of collusion, they are innocent.

Bibliography

BOOKS

Allen, Frederick Lewis. *Only Yesterday*. Harper & Brothers, 1931.

Angell, Norman. *The Great Illusion, 1933*. G.P. Putnam's Sons, 1933.

Beck, L. Adams. *The House of Fulfillment*. T. Fisher Unwin Limited, 1927.

-----. *The Way of Power*. Cosmopolitan Book Corporation, 1927.

Berton, Pierre. *My Country.* McClelland and Stewart, 1987.

Besant, Annie. *Theosophy.* T.C. & E.C. Jack, N.d.

Blavatsky, H.P. *Isis Unveiled.* Theosophical University Press, 1972.

-----. *The Voice of the Silence.* The Chinese Buddhist Research Society, 1927.

Collins, Mabel. *When the Sun Moves Northward.* Theosophical Publishing House, 1917.

Collins, Randall. *The Case of the Philosopher's Ring.* Crown Publishers Inc., 1978.

Colombo, John Robert. *Mysterious Canada.* Doubleday Canada Limited, 1988.

Coue, Emile. *Self Mastery.* George Allen & Unwin Ltd., 1959.

Greenwalt, Emmett A. *The Point Loma Community in California, 1897-1942.* University of California Press, 1955.

Gurdjieff. (with a Forward by Jeanne De Saltzmann). *Views From the Real World.* E.P. Dutton & Co. Inc., 1973.

Hodgins, Jack. *The Invention of the World.* Macmillan, 1977.

Holbrook, Stewart H. *The Golden Age of Quackery.* Macmillan, 1959.

-----. *Murder Out Yonder.* The Macmillan Company, 1941.

Kueshana, Eklal. *The Ultimate Frontier.* The Stelle Group, 1974.

Lillard, Charles. *"Lady with Mask..."* (Victoria) *Times-Colonist,* April 23, 1989.

Lutyens, Lady Emily. *Candles in the Sun.* Rupert Hart-Davis, 1957.

McKelvie, B.A. *Magic, Murder and Mystery.* McKelvie, N.d.

Mowry, George E. (Ed). *The Twenties.* Prentice-Hall, Inc., 1963.

New, W.H. *Articulating West.* New Press, 1972.

Orrmont, Arthur. *Love Cults & Faith Healers.* Ballantine Books, 1961.

Santucci, James A. *"The Aquarian Foundation".* Department of Religious Studies Seminar Paper Series [California State University, Fullerton] No. 40.

Speeth, Kathleen Riordan. *The Gurdjieff Work.* Pocket Books, 1978.

Tillett, Gregory. *The Elder Brother.* Routledge & Keegan Paul, 1982.

Vonnegut Jr., Kurt. *Wampeters, Foma & Granfallons (Opinions).* Dell Publishing Co. Inc., 1976.

White, Stewart Edward. *Secret Harbour.* Grosset & Dunlap, 1926.

-----. *Skookum Chuck.* Grosset & Dunlap, 1925.

-----. *The Unobstructed Universe.* E.P. Dutton & Co. Inc., 1940.

Wilson, Edward Arthur. *Foundation Letters and Teachings [By the Brother, XII].* Sun Publishing Co., 1927.

-----. *The Aquarian Foundation.* Sun Publishing Co., 1927.

-----. *The End of the Days.* The Chalice Press, 1928.

-----. *The Three Truths.* The Chalice Press, 1926.

-----. *Unsigned Letters from an Elder Brother.* L.N. Fowler & Co., N.d.

Wilson, Herbert Emmerson. *Canada's False Prophet.* Simon & Schuster of Canada, Ltd., 1967.

Woods, Richard. *The Occult Revolution.* Herder and Herder, 1971.

MAGAZINES

The Beacon
The Canadian Theosophist
The Chalice
Maclean's Magazine
The Star Weekly Magazine
Saturday Night
The Skipper
The Shoulder Strap
True Police Cases

NEWSPAPERS

Cowichan Leader
Daily Colonist
The Ladysmith Chronicle
Nanaimo Daily Free Press
The Vancouver Daily Province
Vancouver Sun
Saanich Peninsula and Gulf Islands Review

Index

Brother XII

Edited by Camilla Newman
Cover art and design by Barbara Munzar
Book design, map rendering and typesetting by Troy Berg
Set in Palatino, 10/12

This book was designed, typeset and prepared for printing elec-
tronically using ALDUS PageMaker® 3.0 and a QMS-PS 800 Plus
laser printer.

Printed in Canada by Hignell Printing, Winnipeg, Manitoba.

For information about these or other books published by Porcépic
Books, please contact us at 4253 Commerce Circle, Victoria, British
Columbia, Canada, V8Z 4M2